T0302158

iMind

Why has so much of our recent attention been focused on AI while RI is all but forgotten? And why are we spending so much energy debating the future of AI rather than that of its human original? Why can't those who are concerned about AI and those who care about RI talk to one another using a common language?

iMind: Artificial and Real Intelligence is the first comprehensive popular science account of AI and RI. Unique in scope, it discusses the interdisciplinary science of AI, RI, smartphones, smart sensors, microchips, and the brain-mind connection. It explores what is beyond the physical, including mindfulness and spirituality, and how they can impact our wellbeing in the here and now, and how they can help us achieve a healthy and fulfilling old age.

Mohamed I. Elmasry, PhD, FIEEE, FRSC, FCAE, FEIC, is Emeritus Professor of Computer Engineering at the University of Waterloo.

iMind

Artificial and Real Intelligence

Mohamed I. Elmasry

Foreword by
Aileen Burford-Mason, PhD

CRC Press
Taylor & Francis Group
Boca Raton London New York

CRC Press is an imprint of the
Taylor & Francis Group, an **informa** business

Cover image: Alberto GIACOMETTI, Copie d'Abraham (détail de la Maesta di Santa Trinita) d'après Cimabue et buste d'homme, c. 1958, Succession Alberto Giacometti/ADAGP, Paris 2024

First edition published 2025
by CRC Press
2385 NW Executive Center Drive, Suite 320, Boca Raton FL 33431

and by CRC Press
4 Park Square, Milton Park, Abingdon, Oxon, OX14 4RN

CRC Press is an imprint of Taylor & Francis Group, LLC

ISBN: 978-1-032-78221-8 (hbk)
ISBN: 978-1-032-77874-7 (pbk)
ISBN: 978-1-003-48684-8 (ebk)

DOI: 10.1201/9781003486848

Typeset in Optima LT Std
by KnowledgeWorks Global Ltd.

Dedicated to

all who are inspired to enhance human RI in the age of AI.

And to my brother-in-law John Barry, in heaven. To all those everywhere who are suffering from Alzheimer's and other neurodegenerative conditions. To those who may be diagnosed with these conditions in the future and to all their caring loved ones.

Contents

Acknowledgments

Over my long career of more than 50 years as a leading global designer and researcher of advanced microchips used in many applications, including AI, I have always been awed and impressed by the First Designer of all things, G-d Almighty—so impressed that I modeled my work on the brain-mind connection after human RI. I thank G-d for all the great and beautiful designs I have been privileged to study and for the many, many more in this amazing Universe that I have been allowed to enjoy and admire through my own senses.

I thank Dr. Aileen Burford-Mason for all her advice and for writing the Foreword to this book. From the start, she believed in my aspiration to write a genuinely interdisciplinary popular science book on AI and RI—one that is both timely and well-researched.

Established researchers and academics in biochemistry, RI and the human brain-mind like Dr. Burford-Mason and those, like myself, in the field of microchips, AI and smartphones, rarely collaborate. Yet we both have to grapple with these very complex and complementary systems. Closing the knowledge gap between them can reap rich rewards for the wellbeing of individuals and the collective public good.

Perhaps part of the ease and engagement of our collaboration was that it has also been a cross-cultural one—between an Irish-Canadian and an Egyptian-Canadian.

I thank my family and friends who have patiently and supportively listened to me talking about *iMind: Artificial and Real Intelligence* and have steadfastly provided much-needed encouragement and advice.

I thank my friend and long-time editor Pauline Finch, for her patience and for doing an excellent job.

I am also greatly indebted to the excellent team at Routledge, especially to Randi Slack and Lucy McClune.

About the author

Mohamed I. Elmasry

Mohamed Elmasry, PhD, FRSC, FIEEE, FCAE, FEIC is Emeritus Professor of Computer Engineering at the University of Waterloo. He is a leading world expert with more than 50 years of research and industrial consulting experience in Microchips and Artificial Neural Networks (ANNs). He has published 20 books and more than 500 research papers. His students are leaders in both academia and industry; among them, a co-founder of the iconic Blackberry Company (Research in Motion). Dr. Elmasry is a member of the San Francisco-based Center for AI Safety.

Foreword
by Aileen Burford-Mason, PhD

iMind: Artificial and Real Intelligence, the latest book by renowned engineer and academic professor, Mohamed Elmasry, is a fascinating examination of the role Artificial Intelligence (AI) plays in our modern world, and its impact on our present and future lives. Despite the fact that AI has been part of our technological landscape for decades, it's safe to say that until recently most non-technically inclined individuals like myself did not fully grasp the extent to which it had infiltrated our lives and how seamlessly it has been integrated into various aspects of everyday activities.

When I use a search engine such as Google, AI is there, attempting to understand my needs and deliver results that are most relevant to my query. AI is revolutionizing the fields of healthcare and medicine. Already it can analyze X-rays and MRIs many times faster and often more accurately than humans, allowing quicker and more reliable diagnoses. But for all the ways in which AI has made our lives simpler and more efficient, for many it has created a high degree of anxiety. This anxiety is largely grounded in ignorance—a lack of understanding about what AI is, how it works and where it is headed. While we don't need to be experts to use AI, there is an underlying sense of unease about a tool so powerful, that its operation seems shrouded in mystery.

This is where Professor Elmasry's book is so timely and informative. Designed to engage a diverse audience—including general readers curious about the basic scientific principles on which AI is based— *iMind: Artificial and Real Intelligence* explains in everyday language some of the fundamental concepts at the core of AI; from physical hardware like microchips, to applications like machine learning and other tools used for building, training, and operating AI systems.

But *iMind* also emphasizes that the development of artificial neural networks at the heart of AI has depended heavily on an understanding of how the human brain works. In teaching computers how to think, speak and reason approximately like us, we need to remember that the human brain is infinitely more complex than the most sophisticated computer. This is what Professor Elmasry calls Real Intelligence (RI).

The development of RI begins in utero, and can be considered comparable to establishing the hardware set-up on a smartphone. Just as a smartphone is assembled by combining individual hardware components, and relies on the integration of various parts, the human brain develops by assembling neurons and forming intricate neural networks. And just as a smartphone receives its Operating System in the factory, human brains receive their basic operating instructions in the womb.

Where RI deviates from AI is made clear in Professor Elmasry's book. The functioning and efficiency of human neural networks throughout our lives—even their very survival—depend heavily on multiple external inputs, including such basics as adequate nutrition. After birth, throughout childhood, and continuing into adulthood and old age, sensory experiences help build and maintain our neural connections, enhancing learning and cognition.

The brain has extraordinarily high energy needs and consumes glucose, its main energy source, at ten times the rate of other organs. And the harder we work, the more energy the brain requires. Without an adequate supply of glucose, we lose focus and concentration. But AI never tires. It does not get exhausted or stressed and can rapidly analyze vast data sets with an accuracy and rapidity that would be impossible for the human brain. Other factors acquired from our diet, such as vitamins, minerals, proteins, and healthy fats, exert their influence on the brain's neural networks by supporting their survival, efficient functioning, and facilitating communication.

iMind: Artificial and Real Intelligence explores whether or not we are making the best use of our human brains. Are we feeding them adequately? Is our RI receiving the external inputs it needs to optimize its functioning—the nutritional, sensory, and experiential inputs that enhance creativity and perception and reinforce memory? How can we get the best out of technology, using AI to augment and improve our human capacities, while at the same time nurturing and expanding Real Intelligence?

This is a fundamental question for our time, and one that is ably and comprehensively answered in Prof. Elmasry's book.

Aileen Burford-Mason PhD

Toronto

January 2024

Dr. Burford-Mason is a cell biologist and former assistant professor in the Faculty of Medicine, University of Toronto. She is author of *The Healthy Brain: Optimize Brain Power at Any Age* (HarperCollins, 2017), which emphases nutrition as a natural way to achieve optimal mental health and wellness.

Preface

My writings have an astonishing peculiarity; they give more profit according to the manner in which they are read.
(Conference of the Birds, by 12th-century Sufi Master, Farid ud-Din Attar (Attar of Nishapur, 1145 – c.1221))

When I was asked what "i" means in *iMind* … I responded that it signifies all that is good about the human mind—*i*ntelligent, *i*nformative, *i*nstructive, *i*nteresting, *i*nnovative and, above all, *i*maginative.

Why has so much of our recent attention been focused on AI while RI is all but forgotten?

And why are we spending so much energy debating the future of AI rather than that of its human original?

Why can't those who are concerned about AI and those who care about RI talk to one another using a common language?

iMind: Artificial and Real Intelligence is the first comprehensive popular science account of AI and RI. Unique in scope, it discusses the interdisciplinary science of AI, RI, smartphones, smart sensors, microchips, and the brain-mind connection. It explores what is beyond the physical, including mindfulness and spiritually, how they can impact our wellbeing in the here and now, and how they could help us all to achieve a healthy and fulfilling old age.

Today, AI (Artificial Intelligence) has become a household word and a common media headline. Google statistics show that it is searched more than a million times a month (summer, 2023).

In May 2023, mainstream media interviews with Canadian AI "godfather" Professor Geoffrey Hinton of the University of Toronto, a colleague of mine, were read and watched by millions.

According to the New York-based marketing research company Statista (www.statista.com), today (2023) the number of smartphone users is 6.92 *billion*, or 85.95% of the world's entire population. And among those under 30 around the globe, 94% have smartphones. The statistics are mind-boggling—and they will only increase over time.

On the other side of the technology coin, current bestseller lists include popular science-based books dealing with nutrition, aging, wellness, mindfulness, memory, human brains and minds, and physical, mental, or spiritual health.

Can AI Inspire us to enhance our RI? This has become an increasingly important question as our knowledge of both kinds of intelligence advances.

Yet more than three decades ago, Hugh Kenner brilliantly captured the essence of a universal answer in just one sentence in *The Mechanic Muse* (Oxford University Press, 1987):

Technology alters our sense of what the mind does, what are its domains, how characterized and bounded. (Italics added.)

Kenner (1923–2003) was a Canadian literary scholar and professor at University of California, Santa Barbara, Johns Hopkins University, and the University of Georgia.

In this book we are about to explore together the *how* by knowing the *what*.

We will learn about what AI and microchips are; examine the brain-mind connection; the role of aging; and life beyond the physical, including spirituality and mindfulness.

Perhaps, to paraphrase Hugh Kenner, we will alter our own senses of what the mind does.

Mohamed I. Elmasry
Waterloo, Ontario
January, 2024

Introduction

According to the New York-based marketing research company Statista (www.statista.com), today (2023) the current number of smartphone users is 6.92 *billion*, or 85.95% of the world's entire population. And among those under 30 around the globe, 94% have smartphones. The statistics are mind-boggling, and they will only increase over time.

How can we help those young adults make better lifestyle choices with the technologies at their fingertips? How can a greater awareness of Real Intelligence (RI) and Artificial Intelligence (AI) help them continue on in life to a mentally, spiritually, and physically healthier old age?

Smartphones have smart sensors, like cameras and built-in speakers and mics. Do we older folks know how to fully use them? *Without asking our grandkids?*

Similarly, our brain-mind connection uses smart sensors for seeing, hearing, smelling, tasting, touching, talking, etc. Our human processing capabilities operate at a far higher efficiency than today's most advanced AI and with much greater accuracy. But do we know enough about how they work, or how to take the best care of them?

All of our many human sensors should be used more often and more mindfully to enhance our RI and brain-mind connection, not to mention exercising our associated memory. To add such amazing sensors to smartphones is theoretically possible but an extremely expensive proposition, with no guarantee of ever fully replicating what we humans are fortunate to be born with.

Yet computer scientists and microchip experts have worked diligently for the past 80 years to make great strides in emulating a range of human-like brain-mind connections in smart devices. In fact, we have

DOI: 10.1201/9781003486848-1

reached an era of technological innovation never before seen in human history—*never!*

Today, we can communicate virtually anywhere and everywhere, 24/7, using smartphones: via text messaging, email, audio recording, photographs, or in real time with full voice and/or full color video settings.

Today, we can teach and learn anything online, from music to math to cooking … any subject you can name.

We can provide real-time online health care to remote regions largely inaccessible to in-person visits by a doctor, nurse practitioner, or other healthcare professionals, including mental health therapists. We can even measure our brain and/or heart functions second-by-second and send the data to distant specialists.

We can shop and pay for most of our needs online and have our purchases delivered to our doors. Millions of people learned to do this during prolonged COVID-19 lockdowns all over the world and continue to do so for the speed and convenience of it.

Besides working or learning from home online, we can also take part in many virtual recreational and self-care activities as well, such as attending concerts, mindfulness meditation, yoga classes, book clubs, how-to workshops, music or language lessons, and church services.

And every new generation of technology brings us all these opportunities at a *lower cost per function*—an amazing achievement that has never before been possible.

Now, and only now, we can go the full circle. It's time to find more and better ways, for example, to slow down the degenerative process of Alzheimer's disease by learning from AI how to develop our RI associative memories and maintain them through restorative lifestyle choices.

With the amount of supporting knowledge now available, there is no longer any need to wait until complete evidence is presented from neuroscience laboratories, if indeed there can be any point at which we can call this research "complete." Chapter 7 on *Healthy Aging* explores how to enhance our brain functions and refresh them by (would you believe?) *napping*, a simple practice that has long been overlooked, even ridiculed; but not any longer!

Have we now reached the point where science can borrow the concepts of preprogramming and operating systems from AI to complement our understanding of human behavior and find new treatments for mental illness? The potential is promising.

But humans aren't machines, biological or otherwise. We are far better described as multi-dimensional beings with interconnected and even inter-dependent physical, mental, emotional, and spiritual facets. This understanding makes an even stronger case for integrating BTP (*Beyond the Physical*, Chapter 6) elements into our lives—including mindfulness and spirituality to enhance our RI and help the brain-mind connection do a better job taking in care of us.

Humans are impacted by factors such as genetics, upbringing, and lifestyle. We have little control over the first two, but we can significantly influence the third through informed and proactive choices. *iMind: Artificial and Real Intelligence* helps us identify some of these and readers are invited to contribute their own ideas and experiences at iMindNow.co.

iMind addresses an increasingly important interdisciplinary subject by narrowing the knowledge gap between smartphones, AI and microchips, and our human RI, BTP, and holistic brain-mind connections.

For the first time, a non-specialist book describes in compact and accessible form eight decades of research by hundreds of computer scientists, AI developers, microchip experts, biologists, neurologists, psychologists, mindfulness practitioners, and more.

Studying AI and microchips is a difficult subject in itself, but studying RI, the human brain, the human mind, and their myriad connections is even more difficult. In the case of AI and microchips, we know exactly how they work because we designed them. But there are still many mysteries to the design of humans themselves; we may never know *everything* about how we operate!

Chapter 2 on *Understanding Microchips*, and Chapter 3 on *Intelligence: Artificial and Real* deal with basic science and are written for the general public rather than experts. Definitions of specialized terms are listed in the Glossary.

The human brain-mind comes to us fully functional—no assembly or pre-programming needed—but so far we have found no way to ask its Designer any technical questions, much less receive useful responses. So we must rely instead on our inherent designed-in abilities to observe and conduct experiments, which in themselves are limited to doing human subjects no harm.

Studying the brain-mind connection as a software-hardware system has introduced exciting new concepts, like preprogramming, associated memories, and operating systems for managing our body's functions at different hierarchical levels, from single cells to complete organs. Research into rewriting our memories and their functionality could lead, for example, to new treatment concepts for cancer, mental illness, and neurodegenerative conditions like Parkinson's and Alzheimer's disease.

While the brain-mind can be compared to a hardware-software system, this should not mean that studying it cannot be holistic. On the contrary, evidence-based mindfulness and spirituality are essential components in meaningful research.

In Chapters 4, 5, and 6, *iMind: Artificial and Real Intelligence* deals with the most recent brain and mind research, including their complex and fascinating connections.

Chapter 7 is devoted to *Healthy Aging*, an issue as important as climate change, but not receiving the same attention or anywhere near the same political capital being invested in it.

The interdisciplinary brain-mind connection is not new science

In 1975, William Feindel (1918–2014) MD, PhD, Professor of Neurosurgery at McGill University and Director of the Montreal Neurological Institute (MNI), wrote in the Introduction to colleague Dr. Wilder Penfield's *Mystery of the Mind* (Princeton University Press, 1975):

> Perhaps at no previous time in the history of science has there been such widespread interest, as is now evident, in the brain and its function, and how that function relates to human behavior. For compelling and obvious reasons, this topic has always been foremost in the attention of neurologists, neurosurgeons, and psychiatrists. Over many years, as well, the study of the brain has attracted the talents of scientists trained in anatomy, physiology, pathology, and other biological disciplines. Increasing numbers of intellectual émigrés, coming from such fields as mathematics, physics, chemistry, electronics, and computer sciences, have recently added fresh impetus to our exciting researchers in neuroscience.

Prof. Feindel's words proved prophetic. Today in 2023, *iMind: Artificial and Real Intelligence* can be added to his resource list of researchers, microchip experts, AI developers, and mindfulness practitioners.

Explaining RI in AI language

Now let us first explore how to understand AI language through the preprogrammed functions of the infant brain-mind connection.

The fetus in a mother's womb already has a developing brain-mind. In order to grow to full term, its brain is preprogrammed to coordinate vital functions such as breathing, blood pressure, heart rhythm, and digestion. If a fault occurs in any of these operations, the fetus could die.

To survive outside the mother's womb as a baby, the infant brain is also preprogrammed to recognize the mother through hearing her voice, smelling and tasting her milk, and even touching her skin. As a newborn can see very little and cannot yet focus, the brain's preprogrammed facial recognition algorithm is not yet activated.

But the baby quickly learns the skills of searching for the nipple, latching onto it with its mouth, sucking, and swallowing, so that its body can begin the complex involuntary events of digestion and later, excretion. Without language, babies can still effectively communicate by crying to express hunger, pain, or the discomfort of a soiled diaper.

Although an infant's brain is already doing remarkable things to ensure its survival outside the womb, the huge capability of the mature brain-mind is a long way in the future.

At this stage, if the mother is replaced by a new caregiver, a baby may either accept or reject a different source of milk or nourishment, based on its preprogrammed survival algorithms.

When the baby can see, its brain's recognition algorithm is activated and the face of the mother is included. If the infant is then approached by an unfamiliar face, the crying algorithm may activate.

At a certain age the growing baby will use supervised and unsupervised learning algorithms to activate listening and vocalizing, reaching out to grasp things, and balancing as walking is learned. As a toddler and growing child, emotions such as love, joy, fear, and hate are also activated; then come awareness of the self and surroundings, imitation, experimentation, and so on.

Now if an infant could hypothetically survive alone on a desert island, the ability to add acquired skills or Apps to the preprogrammed brain-mind would be much more limited; but the child could theoretically survive through adapting to its surroundings and environment, just as the human-assisted one could. Thus the number of acquired or activated Apps and their complexity depend on upbringing and environment.

If we fast-forward to adulthood, we find that the mature human brain activates preprogrammed Apps, or adds new ones, in response to certain stimuli. And here is where the gap between the human brain-mind and microchip and AI technology widens.

One important brain-mind stimulus is the knowledge we all share that humans inevitably die. Another is that humans, and only humans, are directly responsible for the survival of their species.

Yet another level of human brain-mind complexity is that we are made up of living cells that continually die and need replacement. So everything depends on a manufacturing house called the body, which not only needs to supply itself with the energy to perform its own motor functions but also must supply the brain-mind with nourishment.

In return, the body is controlled by the brain-mind's preprogrammed Apps. But, for better or worse, humans can override those Apps and harm themselves by doing so.

Consider the preprogramming that enables our digestive system to extract nutrients from food.

It starts in the mouth with our teeth, tongue, and saliva. If we fail to chew our food properly, the App that continues digestion in the stomach and gut cannot perform optimally and the body suffers. The brain-mind may tolerate this for some time, but can be permanently damaged if the abuse continues.

Food enters the stomach, then progresses through the small and large intestines, where wastes are gathered and then excreted some six hours later.

The hardware-software coordination that regulates this chain of events even when we're scarcely aware of it is very complicated. Therefore the algorithms must be allowed to perform their programmed functions without interference. If not, complications, even death, can result.

Reverse engineering the brain-mind connection

Here are notes that may help in understanding and reverse-engineering our brain-mind connection. They are not in any special order.

1. The information in smartphones and other AI devices is carried by electrical signals; in the human brain-mind, it is carried by electrical *and* chemical signals.

2. Our brain-mind contains associated memory that is content-dependent, while smartphone/AI memory is mainly randomly stored and randomly accessible.

    Moreover, the smartphone designer and/or user knows precisely where its memory locations are. In the case of the human brain, its exact memory locations are only known to the original Designer and only vaguely known to the user and/or researcher. The human memory is non-volatile; that is, not easily erasable, while a smartphone's memory contents can be saved or deleted at will. Smartphone/AI memory is theoretically unlimited, while that of the human brain-mind is finite, yet designed to be better optimized.

    Smartphone information is saved on memory chips, while the human brain stores it in the interconnections between cells. This gives the brain-mind a very high capacity in a limited space—an engineering miracle not easily imitated.

3. The human brain-mind works in the analog realm of the natural world, but a smartphone must work in the digital domain. Relying on analog-to-digital and digital-to-analog devices results in decreased accuracy and increased energy consumption.

4. The brain physically operates within the 3D space of the human skull, while smartphones can use only the 2D space available from microchips.

5. In smartphone/AI devices, all operations depend on a synchronizing clock, while human brain-mind operations are asynchronously event-driven. To design an asynchronous microchip system is next to impossible.

6. The useful life expectancy for current smartphones is around 10 years, while a healthy brain-mind inside a healthy human body can live for 100 years or longer. Moreover, the human operating system requires much less energy to work at full efficiency than the smartphone/AI.

7. The current emphasis on cutting health care costs due to short-staffing often leaves doctors with inadequate time to talk to patients, especially those suffering with mental health issues. Patients and their families are forced to take more responsibility for educating themselves.

8. We must consider what we mean by science, and by scientific research when studying a complex subject like the human brain-mind, as well as the impact of the research methodologies we follow.

If by "science" we mean traditional empirical fields such as physics and chemistry (often called "hard science" because they are about measurable and calculable entities), this is definitely different from behavioral science, political science, social science, religion and spirituality sciences, etc., which depend on qualitative, observational and experiential information as well as (or sometimes instead of) quantitative and numerical values.

Common to both these broad areas, however, are the creation and application of theories, fact-based supporting evidence, experimentation, observation, modeling, analysis, and correlations. New results must be accepted by a majority of acknowledged experts in the field, not necessarily by *all* experts in the field, and not necessarily by the general public to whom all the decision-making data is rarely available.

These differences and commonalities are important to be aware of when studying the human brain-mind versus machines, such as smartphones and other devices driven by microchips and AI. When dealing with the latter, we do not have to bring religious sciences directly into our studies, except when considering moral issues around the use of AI.

In exploring the human brain-mind, however, we can't ignore the sciences pertaining to religion, faith, and spirituality; to do so would be to deprive our studies of essential and unique elements.

As a general research rule, the higher a system's complexity, the more sciences we need to draw upon; this is where the interdisciplinary factor is invaluable.

In studying AI and microchips, it's enough to use the mathematical sciences, along with their close relatives, physics, and chemistry. For studying the brain-mind—the highest-complexity system of all—we must use math, physics, chemistry, biology, physiology, behavioral science, psychology, social science, environmental science, religion, spirituality, philosophy, and more—a tapestry of interwoven sciences.

Feeding curious young minds

Bringing back a polymath approach to academia could help future generations achieve a much fuller understanding of the human brain-mind. In the "good old days" a university professor was not only a polymath (having an advanced level of knowledge in multiple disciplines, languages and skills) but also an artist, poet, musician, etc. In the past, academia was much more focused on serving and advancing humanity instead of training people for jobs.

It is hoped that this book reaches the hands and minds of high school students, perhaps inspiring some to embrace the polymath approach to learning, and that universities will reintroduce or retain those broad-based but stimulating degree programs that will restore the stature of post-secondary learning.

Thomas Young (1773–1829) was a British polymath who by age 20 knew French, Italian, Hebrew, Arabic, Persian, Turkish and more. By age 26, he was a professor of Natural Philosophy at the Royal Institute, lecturing on acoustics, optics, gravitation, astronomy, heat, electricity, climate, animal life, vegetation, hydrodynamics, music theory, and Egyptian hieroglyphics. Such versatility is unheard of today. In fact, a 2007 biography by Andrew Robinson calls Young "the last man who knew everything."

Another example of a famous polymath was Irish Bishop George Berkeley (1685–1753) who contributed the theory of immaterialism and published *A New Theory of Vision*, where he argued that the brain interprets what the eye sees by associating signals received from all the senses with images already in the memory.

Accidental discoveries are still good discoveries. While a student, British chemist William Perkin (1838–1907) was trying to synthesize quinine, a natural anti-parasitic agent for the treatment of malaria, when he accidentally discovered the first synthetic dye, a shade called mauveine, also known as aniline purple.

Moving into our own era, Dr. Andrew Grove (1936–2016) was an engineer, physicist, scholar, and businessman who is credited with bringing microchips into mass production by co-founding Intel, the world's largest (and still leading) microchip manufacturer.

Grove wrote a number of classic text and reference books in the field, including *Physics and Technology of Semiconductor Devices* (1967) and *High Output Management* (1985). In 2001, he told his personal story in *Swimming Across: A Memoir*, recalling his life before and after immigrating to the United States in 1957 from his birth country of Hungary as a 21-year-old Jewish youth.

I am the proud owner of his *Physics and Technology of Semiconductor Devices*, as it was central to my PhD studies at the University of Ottawa, 1968–1974. I also greatly valued Dr. Grove's second book because I managed, for about 40 years, one of the largest microchip research groups in the world, based at the University of Waterloo. And I can personally relate to his memoir, recalling my own experience of coming to Canada from Egypt as a 24-year-old Muslim Arab youth.

Faith doesn't need any apology in research. It's clear that there is a difference between objectives and the abilities used to reach those objectives. As both faith and research share the common objective or goal of enhancing human wellbeing and that of future generations, mindfulness and spirituality should always be a natural part of our research methodology. Never apologize for faith!

The analogies presented here in exploring parallels between the human brain-mind and microchip/AI-based machines such as computers and smartphones can hopefully be used in research as well as helping to increase knowledge and interest among the general public.

An especially entertaining and informative analogy was presented some 40 years ago by British science historian and BBC TV personality, James Burke (b. 1936) in a one-hour video with animation, comparing the human brain-mind with a 5-star hotel. It's called *The Neuron Suite*. I highly recommend it and it's still available on YouTube at https://www.youtube.com/watch?v=FjxMWQ2dlmQ

Table 1.1 represents the hierarchy of complexity of the four systems explored in this book—AI, the microchip, the brain, and the mind—assigning for comparative purposes values contributing to human wellbeing. The sciences needed to study each system are also included.

Table 1.1 Hierarchy table: complexity, values, and sciences needed

	Complexity	Sciences	Value
1. AI	AI Elements 101	Math Sciences 101	100
	AI Systems 102	Math Sciences 102	1,000
2. Microchip	Microchip Elements 201	Physics 201 Chemistry 201	10K
	Microchip Systems 202	Physics 202 Chemistry 202	100K
3. Brain	Brain Cells 301	Biology 301	1M
	The Brain 302	Biology 302	10M
4. Mind	The Mind YOU 401	Behavior Sciences 401	100M
	The Mind WE 402	Behavior Sciences 402	1B

In each case, complexity comes with many levels, so only two are shown. One is the individual (element) level and the other is the multi-element (or system) level.

The higher complexity of the system or multi-element level stems from the fact that in order to coexist and create a system, a group of elements must have a complex interconnectivity, laws of interdependence, and communication protocols, even though they may lead to instability, uncertainty, and chaotic behavior.

At a system level, studying the impact of time, place, and environment becomes more important in predicting performance than when studying individual elements, one at time.

Any of these systems "exhibits a distinctive property called emergence; roughly described by the common phrase that the action of the whole is more than the sum of the actions of the parts," notes Dr. John H. Holland, Professor of Psychology and Computer Science and Engineering at the University of Michigan in his book *Complexity: A Very Short Introduction* (Oxford University Press, 2014).

In studying and developing AI at the element level, we need mathematical sciences 101; but to study and develop a group of AI Apps we need a correspondingly higher level of mathematical sciences, 102.

Similarly, in studying and developing microchips we need (in addition to the mathematical sciences), physics and chemistry 201 at the individual transistor level—the main building block for microchips—and physics 202 and chemistry 202 at the higher complexity level of microchips.

To get to the level of the human brain, we move up in the hierarchy of complexity. To the sciences mentioned so far, we now add biology 301 at the cellular level and biology 302 at the brain system level. To add to the overall complexity, each of these sciences consists of several branches.

Now we have reached the absolute highest level of complexity—YOU, a single mind as a person; and WE, a group of minds, in a family, a social community, a political structure, or an economic group, etc. Here, we need the help of behavioral sciences, social sciences, political sciences, and even the sciences of religion, faith, philosophy, spirituality, etc.

If we attach a value according to the levels of complexity (and replacement costs in case of damage), just for discussion purposes, let us assume a starting value at the lowest level of complexity of 100 for a single AI App, and moving up by a factor of 10 in value from one level of complexity to the next. Eventually, we reach 1,000,000 for the brain at the cellular level,

10,000,000 for the brain at the system level, 100,000,000 million for a single mind and … one *billion* for a system of interacting minds.

At such a high level of complexity, both reductionist and holism methodology are needed. Here, we cannot afford to deny or ignore the role of religious sciences, mindfulness, and spirituality—all are of critical importance in studying the mind.

Chapter summaries

Chapter 2 Understanding microchips

> The number of transistors on a microchip doubles about every two years.
>
> (Moore's Law, 1965)

In this chapter, we review the history of microchips, discuss how they're made, and explore both differences and similarities between microchips and the human brain. Does Moore's Law still hold true 60 years later in 2023?

Chapter 3 Intelligence—artificial and real

> What we want is a machine that can learn from experiences.
>
> (Alan Turing, 1947)

Here, we address the controversy about AI; what AI is; supporting sciences for AI research; what RI is; and how to build an artificial fruit-fly.

Chapters 4 and 5 The brain-mind connection, I and II

> Mind, meaning by that thoughts, feelings, reasoning, and so on, is difficult to bring into the class of the physical things. Physiology, a natural science, tends to be silent about all outside the physical.
>
> (Sir Charles Sherrington, 1932 Nobel laureate in
Physiology or Medicine)

In these two chapters, we explore the brain and its smart sensors, its interconnection and memory, its anatomy and all the elements that hold it together.

And we then move up to a higher degree of complexity, to the human mind, RI and how its operations differ from AI Apps. We consider the role of sleep, dreams, and humor in the mind—none of which can be duplicated in AI.

Chapter 6 Beyond the physical

> True religion is real living with all one's soul, with all one's goodness.
> (Albert Einstein, 1921 Nobel laureate in Physics)

In this chapter, we review advances in mindfulness and spirituality and how they can help build and maintain a healthy RI and brain-mind connection.

Chapter 7 Healthy aging—a travel guide

> I have one life and one chance to make it count for something.
> (Former American President Jimmy Carter (b. 1924),
> 2002 Nobel Peace Prize laureate)

This chapter delves into achieving healthy aging at the individual level by adopting more mindful lifestyle choices, and at a collective societal level by advocating for and implementing age-friendly policies.

Chapter 8 The future—a balancing act

> Human wisdom begins with the recognition of one's own ignorance.
> (Socrates (c. 470–399 BCE), ancient Greek philosopher)

Here we extrapolate from our current knowledge, or ignorance, projecting forward into the next 10 or 20 years.

For further reading

Anderson, John R. *How Can the Human Mind Occur in the Physical Universe?* Oxford University Press, 2007.

Bar-Yam, Yaneer and Ali A. Mini, eds. *Unifying Themes in Complex Systems, Volume II: Proceeding of the Second International Conference on Complex Systems*. Perseus, 2004.

Belofsky, Nathan. *Strange Medicine: A Shocking History of Real Medical Practices Through the Ages*. Penguin, 2013.

Bloom, Paul. *Psych: The Story of the Human Mind*. HarperCollins, 2023.

Burke, James. *Circles: 50 Round Trips Through History, Technology, Science, Culture*. Simon & Schuster, 2000.

Bury, J.B. *A History of Freedom of Thought*. Williams, 1800.

Bynum, William. *The History of Medicine: A Very Short Introduction*. Oxford University Press, 2008.

Calvin, William H. *A Brain for All Seasons: Human Evolution and Abrupt Climate Change*. University of Chicago, 2002.

Calvin, William H. *How Brains Think: Evolving Intelligence, Then and Now*. Basic, 1996.

Cobb, Matthew. *The Idea of the Brain: A History*. Profile, 2021.

Davies, Paul. *The Mind of God: The Scientific Basis for a Rational World*. Simon & Schuster, 1992.

Eddington, Arthur Stanley. *The Nature of the Physical World*. MacMillan, 1929.

Epictetus, c. 90 CE. *The Art of Living: The Classical Manual on Virtue, Happiness, and Effectiveness*. Harper Collins, 1944.

Fromm, Erich. *Psychoanalysis and Religion*. Yale, 1950.

Greene, Brian. *Until the End of Time: Mind, Matter, and Our Search for Meaning in an Evolving Universe*. Knopf, 2020.

Kant, Immanuel. *Groundwork of the Metaphysic of Morals*. Harper, 1948.

Laslett, Peter, comp. *The Physical Basis of Mind: A Series of Broadcast Talks*. Blackwell, 1950.

Le Fanu, James. *Why Us: How Science Rediscovered the Mystery of Ourselves*. Harper, 2010.

Matthews, Dale A. and Connie Clark. *The Faith Factor: Proof of the Healing Power of Prayer*. Penguin, 1998.

Moscovitch, Morris, ed. *Infant Memory: Its Relation to Normal and Pathological Memory in Humans and other Animals*. Plenum, 1984.

Nadler, Spencer. *The Language of Cells: A Doctor and His Patients*. Vintage, 2002.

Nicolelis, Miguel. *Beyond Boundaries: The New Neuroscience of Connecting Brains with Machines and How it will Change our Lives*. Times, 2011.

Passingham, Richard. *Cognitive Neuroscience*. Oxford University Press, 2016.

Rathbun, Ron. *The Way is Within: A Spiritual Journey*. Quiscince, 1994.

Salmon, C. Wesley. *Four Decades of Scientific Exploration*. Foreword by Paul Humphreys. University of Pittsburgh, 1989.

Smuts, Jan Christiaan. *Holism and Evolution*. Macmillan, 1926.

Weiner, Johnathan. *Long for This World: The Strange Science of Immortality*. HarperCollins, 2010.

Weiner, Johnathan. *Time, Love, Memory: A Great Biologist and His Quest for the Origin of Behavior*. Vintage, 1999.

Zahara, Elie. *Why Science Needs Metaphysics: A Plea for Structural Realism*. Open Court, 2007.

Understanding microchips

The story

In our digital age, where microchips dominate numerous electronic applications, billions of people are able to compute and communicate 24 hours a day using mobile smartphones that cost *per function* a fraction of what they did less than a generation ago.

All this is nothing short of a modern miracle, one as spectacular as that of Moses parting the Red Sea.

Unlike the Biblical one, however, this technological miracle was no solo act; it came about through the talent and innovation of nine remarkable people.

Three were pioneers of modern computer architecture that propelled the 20th-century "information revolution"; another three were behind the discovery of the transistor, the ancestor of electronic miniaturization; and three more developed methods to mass-produce transistors by the billions in microchips, which has become the most important technology industry of the 21st century.

Back in 1945, John von Neumann (1903–1957) was the first to explain that a computer's basic architecture must consist of a processor, a memory, and an input/output device. For the past 70 years, computer engineering and science students have been taught the von Neumann approach to digital information architecture.

Alan Turing (1912–1954) is credited as being the first scientist to articulate that the human brain can be considered a computer. To demonstrate his theory, he built the iconic "Turing machine" to mimic brain memory and response functions.

DOI: 10.1201/9781003486848-2

Claude Shannon (1916–2001) mathematically developed the principles of information theory to aid in the design of digital communication channels, on and off the microchip.

Following those first pioneers, we celebrate three scientists behind the discovery of a miniature semiconductor switch, now universally known as the transistor.

William Shockley (1910–1989), John Bardeen (1908–1991), and Walter Brattain (1902–1987) were all awarded the 1956 Nobel Prize in Physics for "their researches on semiconductors and their discovery of the transistor effect."

If it were not for the next trio of brilliant minds, however, the transistor might well have remained hidden within the research world of scientists and engineers.

But in 1968 Andrew Grove (1936–2016), Robert Noyce (1927–1990), and Gordon Moore (1929–2023) co-founded Intel (short for Integrated Electronics) which quickly became the world's leading manufacturer of microchips, and still is today. Countless home and office computers bear the familiar "Intel Inside" sticker, verifying their authentic components.

The lives of these nine great men have been the subject of many books, of which the following are among the best-known:

The Man from the Future: The Visionary Life of Jon von Neumann, by Ananyo Bhattacharya.

(Norton, 2022)

Turing's Cathedral: The Origins of the Digital Universe, by George Dyson.

(Pantheon, 2012)

A Mind at Play: How Claude Shannon Invented the Information Age, by Jimmy Soni and Rob Goodman.

(Simon & Schuster, 2017)

Broken Genius: The Rise and Fall of William Shockley, the Creator of the Electronic Age, by Joel N. Shurkin.

(MacMillan, 2006)

The Intel Trinity, by Michael S. Malone.

(HarperCollins, 2014)

We don't invent, we discover

"There can be no doubt that the difference between the mind of the lowest man and that of the highest animal is immense," said Charles Darwin in 1859. "Man may be excused for feeling some pride at having risen, though not through his own exertions, to the very summit of the organic scale, and the fact of his having risen, instead of having been aboriginally placed there, may give him some hope for a still higher destiny in the distant future."

Less than 200 years later, the distant future Darwin hoped for in 1859 is here and among its once-imagined features are the realities of advanced microchip technology and its application in AI Apps and smartphones.

Today's young people use smartphones far more fluently than their parents, yet know little about any great scientists, apart from Einstein and Darwin.

The inspiring life story of Andrew S. Grove, told in his beautiful memoir *Swimming Cross* (Winner Books, 2001) could be the inspiration for a feature-length movie. He was born in Budapest, Hungary, during the 1930s into a middle-class Jewish family which survived the Nazi occupation and Russian bombing, only to endure a succession of repressive Communist governments.

In June 1956, a popular Hungarian uprising was crushed and Soviet troops occupied the nation. More than 200,000 Hungarians escaped to the West. Young Andrew Grove was among them. That year, he arrived in the US at age 20 and by 1963 had earned his PhD.

Four years later, Grove wrote the important university text *Physics and Technology of Semiconductor Devices* (Wiley, 1967), while he was the head of the Surface and Device Physics Section at Fairchild Semiconductor Research and Development Laboratory, and lecturer with the University of California at Berkeley.

In 1968, he left Fairchild to co-found Intel. He later wrote the bestselling *High Output Management* (Vintage, 1985), articulating his style of management at Intel, taking it from a Silicon Valley start-up to an international giant in manufacturing microchips.

Did you know?

Without microchips, which are the hardware that runs Apps in all our computing and communication equipment, we would not have smartphones, or any portable devices. Most importantly, we wouldn't have AI at all.

Intel

Intel's Gordon Moore made the historic 1965 prediction—famously dubbed "Moore's Law"—that the number of transistors on a microchip would double every 18–24 months, allowing an entire computer to be designed and manufactured on a single chip.

Increasing the number of transistors on one microchip was achieved by reducing both their size and the distance between them. This increase in miniaturization allowed more processing functions to be packed onto each chip, which in turn accelerated the speed of their operation due to the shorter distances electrical signals had to travel.

But higher processing speeds raised two serious problems. First, the greater power dissipation in ever-shrinking spaces created too much heat, necessitating fans to cool the microchip—a bad idea for mobile devices like smartphones.

The second problem was that microchips needed higher energy to function, hence the need for frequent charging—another bad idea for battery-operated mobile phones.

But both problems were eventually overcome with the development of innovative circuit and system techniques. Here, credit goes to Professor Mohamed Elmasry and his team of gifted graduate students over the past 50 years at the University of Waterloo in Waterloo, Ontario, Canada.

In a remarkably short time, the physical distance between transistors on a microchip was dramatically reduced from 10 μm, to 1 μm, to 0.01 μm, or 1,000 times smaller than the diameter of a human hair.

Throughout its history, Intel has been a model for high-tech companies that not only manufacture but also invest heavily in research. The entire Intel philosophy of continual advancement is summed up in its motto, "Quick or Dead."

When a competing start-up called Advanced Micro Devices (AMD, founded in 1969) challenged Intel's market share by introducing a new microprocessor microchip, former Intel chair and CEO Craig Barrett (b. 1939), sent a succinct hand-written memo to all employees, stating: "We won't let that happen again."

In 1997, Intel released a new microchip that shattered Moore's Law, one that could double the number of transistors it carried in only nine months!

With Intel in the lead, the microchip industry set the world's gold standard: for the first time in industrial history, it proved that every new generation of microchips would cost less per function.

And, not surprisingly, Intel was the driving force that transformed a 100-km stretch of land south of San Francisco (once known as the Prune Capital of America) into the iconic Silicon Valley, home to the highest concentration of microchip, smartphone, software, and electronics industries in the world.

Silicon Valley's rise to fame and household-word status began back in 1954 when transistor pioneer William Shockley moved from Bell Labs on the East Coast to Palo Alto, California, to manufacture his new semiconductor device. There, he founded Fairchild Semiconductors, the direct ancestor of Intel.

The ultimate success of Silicon Valley as an incubator of so many high technology companies, however, is credited to Dr. Frederick Terman (1900–1982), a renowned Professor of Electronics at Stanford University. Terman earned his PhD from MIT in 1924. He was Dean of Engineering at Stanford from 1944 to 1958 and University Provost from 1955 to 1965.

As early as 1938, Terman encouraged two promising young graduate students, William Hewlett and David Packard, to create a company to manufacture and market an electronic oscillator device they had designed under his supervision. From its modest beginnings in a one-car garage, a giant was born—the Hewlett-Packard Company.

Another of Frederick Terman's many contributions to the microelectronics industry was The Stanford Research Park, founded in 1951 as a first-of-its-kind joint initiative between Stanford University and the city of Palo Alto, California. The University of Waterloo and the City of Waterloo were the first in Canada to adopt Terman's model.

Dr. Mohamed Elmasry, University of Waterloo emeritus professor and author of this book, was fortunate to know Terman, who praised his research. Elmasry also used Terman's classic textbook on microelectronics during his undergraduate studies at Cairo University (1960–1965) and later during graduate studies at the University of Ottawa (1968–1974).

How are microchips made?

But just how are microchips made, and why are they so important? The answer falls into two complex areas—the design of the microchip itself and its manufacture.

Both aspects are based on advanced science and engineering, both are difficult to accomplish successfully, and both need highly qualified professionals in those fields. Without exaggeration, the effort and skill needed are comparable to putting a human on the Moon!

To establish a design facility for microchips you need not only outstanding talent, but sufficient capital to attract that talent. You also need to acquire sophisticated state-of-the-art CAD (Computer Aided Design) software to assist designers in their highly detailed and complex work. Microchip designers must know all aspects of the application they are designing for, along with their associated sciences, which involves a very wide range of skills and experience.

For example, the application task could be designing a text-to-speech processer for the Arabic language (one of the most difficult to digitally process), a facial image recognition system to be used in airports or numerous other security-sensitive spaces, a general-purpose computer, or a high-density fast access memory storage device.

Billions of investment dollars are also needed to acquire the physical manufacturing equipment, in addition to paying for an army of engineers, technologists, operators, administrators, and support workers.

This is why many countries like Egypt and Canada have advanced design houses for microchip technology, but much less in the way of bricks-and-mortar commercial manufacturing facilities.

Real-world fact

It costs about 1,000 times more in initial capital to manufacture microchips than it does to finance their design.

To be fab or fabless, that is the question!

Some giant telecommunications companies, such as Qualcomm (founded 1985 in San Diego, California), chose not to build their own microchip manufacturing facilities: they are called "fabless," as they design and market components, but outsource their fabrication. Other tech giants like Samsung are "fab," having their own design and manufacturing facilities all under one corporate roof.

In 2022 (the most recent year for available figures), the two leading areas for microchip use were logic functions (including microprocessors), which accounted for 23% of applications, and memory chips coming a close second at 22%. In the consumer market (where you and I purchase our devices) the top two microchip-based products were computers at 32% and communication devices, another close second at 31%.

Peter Lim Tze Cheng in his 2022 book *What I learnt about Semicon and EMS: A Sharing of my Views on the Industry*, provides an excellent current overview of the microchip and the EMS industries. EMS stands for Electronic Manufacturing Services, or companies that build end-product parts for devices such as smartphones.

Microchips come in two types. The first includes general-purpose and memory microchips, used in manufacturing computing or communications systems.

The second type is special-purpose microchips, designed to do very specific and often complex tasks, such as converting speech into text and vice-versa.

Designing microchips

The design of a microchip begins with knowing its intended function, as the final product will have to answer the real-world question: *What is this microchip supposed to do?* Next, the designer needs to know the technology that the microchip will be manufactured into, including all the advantages and potential disadvantages of that application.

Once those parameters are established, the actual design process begins with determining the speed at which the microchip will run; the faster, the better, as higher speed will allow it to do more in less time.

The next step is to calculate the chip's energy requirements. In this case, the least possible energy uptake is better, as energy consumption impacts how often one must recharge the battery in mobile or portable devices such as smartphones, tablets, and laptops.

A third essential design criterion is to measure how much power the microchip will dissipate as heat. Again, less is better and will determine if an onboard fan is needed to keep the microchips in a device cool enough to operate efficiently.

Finally, the designer must arrange the microchips to occupy as small a physical area as possible, in order to keep manufacturing costs down.

So, the clever designer must develop a microchip that is *fast, energy-conserving, cool, and small!* Achieving all four criteria in one miniature component is not an easy task.

With 50 years of development progressing through multiple generations, microchip design has continued to advance. Not only have they become faster, more energy-efficient, cooler, and smaller; but they have also become increasingly sophisticated, able to perform more specialized functions than ever before.

But—and it is a big but—there *is* a theoretical limit to the concept of optimal functionality. And it has been comfortably reached from time immemorial in none other than the design of the human brain. You see where we are going?

With that picture in mind, let us return to the story of microchips. Once designed how, exactly, are they manufactured?

Real-world fact

The capacity of microchips made of silicon is approaching its physical limits.

The silicon age

To tell this part of the story we must rewind from our present context in the Silicon Age back to the early Iron Age.

We may think of iron as the metal that dominated the era of trains and bridges, especially the accomplishments of Britain's 19th-century Victorian engineers, many of whose structures and infrastructures have weathered the tests of time. However, the earliest iron tools were found in Egyptian tombs dating from around 3500 BCE, preceding the official Iron Age of 1200–600 BCE by a very long margin.

Today's microchip manufacturers depend heavily on silicon, an amazingly versatile element that has existed in abundance ever since the earth was formed.

As a crystalline solid found in clay, granite, quartz, and sand, silicon is a natural semiconductor. Identified as a distinct element in 1854, it was first used extensively in manufacturing transistors. When it is oxidized into glass it is a good insulator. In fact, ancient Egyptians oxidized silicon-bearing rocks and sand to produce ornamental glass beads.

On the Periodic Table, silicon belongs to the group of elements with an atomic number of 14. Carbon and Germanium are also in the same group.

Today, silicon is most easily obtained in large quantities from sand, which must be purified for use in microchip manufacturing. This ever-growing industry is expected to be worth more than $1,000 *billion* by 2030.

In research

Scientists are already exploring how to make non-silicon microchips, including research into biological materials.

What was life like before microchips?

Vacuum tubes, invented by J. A. Fleming back in 1904, were used to build the first widely used electronic equipment, including radio, TV, and computers, long before the dawn of the microchip era. Microchips turned electronics into microelectronics and made mobile devices possible.

Microchips control the flow of electrons as they move around in solids, while vacuum tubes control the flow of electrons in a sealed container, much like an incandescent light bulb. Vacuum tubes were bulky, generated a lot of heat, didn't adapt to miniaturization, and their lifespan was much shorter than that of solid-state devices.

Microchips—the supply chain

The first supply chain process in microchip production is the essential step of converting silica from its natural state in sand into ultrapure single-crystal silicon in the form of extremely thin wafers, about 700 μm thick and ranging from 6 to 12 in. in diameter.

Although there are relatively few suppliers of these silicon wafers, they are all very big players in the industry.

Making microchips is such an exacting process that they must be manufactured in a clean-air environment, cleaner than the most sophisticated hospital operating rooms.

The design information for a given microchip is repeated precisely 100 times to produce the final product. Even the smallest dust speck falling on a single silicon wafer will cause the microchip to malfunction. Each silicon wafer can hold anywhere from 100 microchips to thousands.

Each silicon wafer is rigorously tested to determine the ratio of good microchips to the total number of chips; this resulting figure is called the "yield." For manufacturing costs to be profitable, the yield per wafer must be as high as possible. The bigger the area of individual microchips, the lower the yield.

Testing individual microchips while they are still on the silicon wafer is a sophisticated automated process. Once testing is complete, microchips are cut out from their wafer and the good ones are packaged and labeled according to how and where they will be used.

More expensive than pure gold

Microchips are rigorously tested before being shipped to customers such as smartphone manufacturers. Now this amazing product has reached the point where raw sand has been transformed into functioning microchips; by weight, they are literally more expensive than pure gold.

The ancients' love for gold as a beautiful metal that resists tarnish, erosion, and aging, is well known. For centuries, alchemists worked hard to convert sand and other elements into gold, but without success. The ancient Egyptians used gold to make funereal masks for mummified celebrities, such as the iconic young Pharaoh Tutankhamun, to protect their faces so they would be recognized in the afterlife.

Close-up fact

By weight, microchips are more expensive than the purest refined gold.

Humans have progressed from the Stone Age to the Iron Age, and now we live in the Silicon Age. From the beginning of human tool-making around

2.6 million years ago, stone was the most accessible and effective material. Around 1200 BCE, iron was discovered, an element with greater strength than humans had yet encountered.

Even today, when stronger materials are available, our language retains phrases that refer to iron as a measure of power: the Iron Cross, Iron Lady, Iron Curtain, etc. During the 1850s, at the height of Victorian civil engineering accomplishments, it was discovered that adding other elements to iron produced steel, an even tougher and more versatile structural building material. At the start of the 21st century, the annual world market for steel was estimated to be worth about $500 billion.

Why silicon?

The Periodic Table, introduced in 1899 and containing all the elements known to science, is managed by the International Union of Pure and Applied Chemistry (IUPAC).

See, for example, *The Elements: A Very Short Introduction*, by Philip Ball (Oxford University Press, 2002), who writes:

> Silicon occupies that curious no man's land in the Periodic Table where metals (to the left) give way to non-metals (to the right) … (it) is not a metal, but it does conduct electricity—albeit poorly. It is a semiconductor.

Silicon's electrical conductivity can be slightly increased or decreased by adding other elements. Arsenic atoms have one *more* electron than silicon, so adding arsenic to silicon adds extra negatively charged electrons which increase silicon's conductivity, turning it into "n-type silicon."

Likewise, boron atoms have one *less* electron than silicon. Adding boron to silicon adds missing electrons, called "holes" that can also carry a positive charge, hence the name "p-type silicon."

When an n-type silicon atom comes in contact with a p-type silicon atom, they can conduct electric current in one direction only, thus creating what is called a "p-n junction diode." But a sandwiched arrangement of n-p-n or p-n-p silicon atoms creates a bipolar transistor, the building-block of many microchips. See for example the first book on the subject, *Digital Bipolar Integrated Circuits* by Mohamed Elmasry (Wiley, 1983).

From the Big Bang theory to the band theory of solids

When Einstein was asked to explain his theory of relativity in a few words, he replied that it would take him three days. He might have added that unless his questioners had a good understanding of physics and mathematics, he would not be able to do it at all!

Metals, like gold, conduct electricity easily; silicon dioxide (glass) is an insulator that doesn't conduct electricity; and silicon is a *semiconductor*. The three levels of conduction in these three materials play a major role in microchips. Conduction consists of the motion of electrons. Thus conduction is possible only if we can influence the kinetic (movement) energy of an electron.

The energy band theory of solids, which is part of quantum mechanics, gives us an analytical tool to calculate how much of an electrical field we can apply to move electrons around. Another way electrons can move in solids is by diffusion; that is, moving from regions of high concentration to those of low concentration.

Interestingly, the energy band theory of solids states that electrons in solids can have bands of energy levels. These energy bands are separated by regions called "forbidden gaps" that the electrons can't possess. When enough negatively charged electrons move in the same direction, the result is an electrical current in the *opposite* direction. This happens because, as an electron moves, it leaves an empty space behind called a "hole" (like a wake) that another electron can occupy. Thus the movement of holes also creates a current and both currents go in the same direction.

Using the transistor as a switch or gate to control these currents in networks of circuits (millions of them!) can do amazing things, including processing and storing information, communicating audio and video signals, and performing AI algorithms.

Niels Bohr (1885–1962), the Danish physicist who received the 1922 Nobel Prize in Physics, is credited with discovering the atomic structure of solids, hence its value to the design and manufacturing of microchips. Bohr is known chiefly among microchip specialists, while Big Bang theorists, like the late great Stephen Hawking (1942–2018) have become household names. On October 7, 1965, on what would have been Bohr's 80th birthday, the University of Copenhagen Theoretical Physics Institute was re-named the Niels Bohr Institute.

26

From analog to digital

I consider myself blessed to have been raised, educated, and drawn to a teaching and research career at the dawn of what I consider the most interesting and exciting era of technology. There has never been anything like it before in all of human history. *Never.*

I was born in 1943, just four years before the discovery of the transistor in 1947.

I completed my undergraduate Electrical Engineering degree at Cairo University in 1965, on the cusp of integrated circuit (IC) development and just when the concept of "information theory" was first being formalized.

The moment was right: I fell in love with ICs and decided to do PhD research in this brand new field in Canada, at the University of Ottawa. Following my PhD, I worked for BNR (Bell Northern Research) in Ottawa, developing new ICs for the telecommunications industry.

In 1974, I moved to the University of Waterloo to continue researching digital ICs and systems, soon combining my research with teaching. After a 50-year career, my peers honored me as the field's leading contributor in IC and systems design.

Over that time, I published multiple books and hundreds of research papers and acquired a number of patents, all while teaching, mentoring, and supervising thousands of undergrad and graduate students.

One of my UW students co-founded Waterloo's iconic Research in Motion (RIM) Company, which produced the world's first mobile wireless device, the BlackBerry. In 2023 it became the subject of a critically acclaimed feature-length film directed by Matt Johnson.

In 2023 at the age of 80, as an active Emeritus Professor of Computer Science and Engineering at UW, I am still engaged in research with my former PhD graduates and their own graduate students.

Close-up fact

Today, more microchips are used to process and store digital information than are used for storing analog information *and* for converting analog-to-digital or digital-to-analog.

The original story

But my story, like that of every other microchip researcher, didn't actually start during the mid-1960s. It all began in ancient times with three human needs:

1. To communicate.
2. To compute.
3. To record and preserve information.

All three emerged once humans had found ways to consistently meet their basic needs of eating, drinking, having shelter, and propagating their species. Having achieved survivability, they turned their attention to conveying information to one another, calculating how to do things, and recording and preserving useful knowledge.

To communicate, humans developed oral languages, later devising ways to inscribe spoken words as written symbols. As written language advanced, it allowed people to give and receive orders and information over long distances, as well as to record important events. To build structures, however, they had to become even more specialized by developing mathematics, which resulted in the creation of tools for measurement and computation.

In extending the distances over which oral communication could travel, people enhanced their voices through the use of aids such as drums, horns, bells, or other percussive sounds with far-reaching acoustic properties. In writing, which began with the laborious task of carving on stone or making impressions on clay tablets, people then discovered how to make light, durable sheets from the papyrus plant. It became one of the world's first papers, which made recording and storing records much easier and more accessible. Writing complemented the invention of mechanical tools used in the computation of angles and distances.

All of these accomplishments happened in an analog world. This is because humans communicate, measure, and compute using analogies, or concepts that compare one thing with another in order to explain both basic and complex ideas.

Many analog developments are still familiar to us in our largely digital world:

1. Landline (wired-in) telephones and radio signals communicate analog information.

2. Phonograph discs and magnetic tape contain recorded analog information and music.
3. The slide rule and abacus are mechanical devices that compute analog mathematical data.

The transition from the analog age with its first mechanical devices, to the electronic age with its digital devices is reviewed in photos on *The Calculator Site* (free) at www.thecalculatorsite.com. This useful resource ranges from Egyptian handheld calculators in 2000 BCE that used beads to represent numerical functions, to hand-held electronic calculators, introduced by Hewlett-Packard in the early 1970s.

Paul E. Ceruzzi's *Computing: A Concise History* (MIT Press, Essential Knowledge Series, 2012) provides a good overview. For a current reference, see also *The History of Computing: A Very Short Introduction* by Doron Swade (Oxford University Press, 2022).

The great electronics breakthrough happened in 1947 when Bell Labs scientists John Bardeen and Walter Brattain, under the leadership of William Shockley, discovered the transistor—a solid-state device that can act as an on-off switch—which won the three Americans the 1956 Nobel Prize in Physics.

After discovering the point contact (on-off) transistor, the trio went on to develop the junction field effect transistor (JFET) in 1953. But what really accelerated the progress of solid-state electronics was the co-discovery in 1959 of the MOSFET (Metal Oxide Semiconductor Field Effect Transistor) by Mohamed (John) Atalla (1924–2009) and Dawon Kahng (1931–1992), also from Bell Labs. MOSFET transistors proved more versatile in many applications as they operate efficiently over a wider range of currents.

About the same time, American mathematician Claude Shannon developed a theory demonstrating how an analog signal can be coded to a digital signal using only the values of zero and one, and that it could be transmitted accurately over a wired (physical) *or* wireless channel.

Combining the transistor as a practical switch with Shannon's digital coding information theory marked the birth of a research era unprecedented in human history.

Progress then took an exponential leap ahead with the development of ICs by Jack Kilby (1923–2005) at Texas Instruments, who created and patented the first prototypes, which earned him the 2000 Nobel Prize in Physics.

As their name suggests, ICs were such a major breakthrough because they could potentially carry complete circuits and systems (rather than single transistors) on a single microchip.

From a single transistor on a single chip to the seemingly infinite potential of hundreds of millions within barely half a human generation—this was dramatic progress indeed, and deserved a new name in the field, Very Large Scale Integration (VLSI).

VLSI became a passion for Mohamed Elmasry and many of his students at the University of Waterloo, where in 1980 he founded the school's VLSI Circuit and System Research Group, one of the largest and most generously-funded of its kind in the world. For more than 40 years, Elmasry's dynamic group contributed major developments to VLSI technology, especially that of high-speed low-power VLSI systems. It is these systems that made possible the billions of smartphones being used all over the world to send trillions of messages every single day.

Following in the footsteps of Jack Kilby were Robert Noyce, Gordon Moore, and Andrew Grove, who successfully commercialized ICs by founding the giant Intel microchip manufacturing company in 1968. Their story is told in Michael S. Malone's *The Intel Trinity* (HarperCollins, 2014).

Did you know?

The MOS (Metal Oxide Semiconductor) transistor—building-block of our current microchips—was non-existent just 70 years ago.

Computer-on-a-chip? What a revolutionary idea!

In 1971, Intel introduced its model 4004, the world's first commercially available microprocessor. It was followed by a succession of increasingly powerful microprocessors. The world's largest smartphone companies also began developing their own to meet an ever-growing demand. These super microchips, partnered with high-density memory chips, have continued to fuel a plethora of new smartphone functions and apps. The sky's the limit— well, almost.

Since digital devices like smartphones and computers must interact with humans, who are analog beings, it quickly became necessary to introduce interfaces and digital language translators. Some of these early tools included a "mouse" whose first prototype was built in 1964 by engineer Bill English from a concept developed in 1961 by Doug Engelbart. Next, touch pads became familiar, along with A/D and D/A (Analog-to-Digital and Digital-to-Analog) signal processing. Then came voice-to-text and text-to-voice signal processing.

But with all these innovations, scientists and engineers have yet to succeed in designing machines that can process purely analog signals, or teach humans to talk, write and think digitally!

Did you know?

The first commercial computer to be manufactured on a single microchip was called a microprocessor or CPU (Central Processing Unit), and was pioneered by Intel in 1971.

Very Large Scale Integrated (VLSI) systems

As we've mentioned, VLSI microchips are the major development responsible for the numerous features in your smartphone.

These amazing microchips can accommodate millions of transistors and other components, making it possible to design microchips that act as transmitters, receivers, high-density memory storage, or as stand-alone microprocessors. And they can be packed into ever-smaller mobile devices, all while consuming so little energy and generating so little heat that they don't need cooling fans.

Yet when compared to the systems existing within the human brain, the impressive design power of VLSI microchip technology is still at a very modest level.

It would be an understatement to say that the levels of human brain integration are manifold. The human brain is designed to perform multiple computation and communication functions per second amid a noisy external environment where it can often access only approximate information. Yet it operates with remarkable accuracy and energy efficiency for most or all of an average human's lifetime.

Brainware Large-Scale Integration (BLSI)

This astonishing comparison led to another new research field, BLSI or Brainware Large-Scale Integration, an energy-efficient brain-inspired study of computing. One area of its application is image processing, where information is represented by a random stream of bits called the Bernoulli Sequence. Computation is stochastically (randomly, but measurably) performed in a domain where probabilities are represented by random bit sequences.

An excellent reference on this subject is *Stochastic Computing: Techniques and Applications*, edited by Warren J. Gross and Vincent C. Gaudet (Springer, 2019).

Also, in the *IEEE Transaction on Neural Networks* (September 2003), S. Sato et al. reported on the implementation of a new neurochip, using stochastic computing logic.

Because the microchip designer must deal with the transistor as the individual building-block of a circuit system, he or she must understand its physics right down to the atomic level. The lack of such understanding can only lead to bad design. The same density of detail holds true in studying the human brain.

For example the "father of neuroscience," Oxford professor Sir Charles Scott Sherrington (1857–1952), maintained that the physiology of nervous reactions could be studied from three main points. In his classic textbook *The Integrative Action of The Nervous System* (Yale, 1906), the 1932 Nobel winner in Physiology or Medicine writes:

> In the first place, nerve-cells, like all other cells lead individual lives—they breathe, they assimilate, they dispense their own stores of energy, they repair [themselves] …; each in short, a living unit with its nutrition more or less centered in itself. Secondly, nervous cells present a feature so characteristically developed in them as to be especially theirs; they have in exceptional measure the power to spatially transmit (conduct) states of excitement (nerve-impulses) generated within them. A third aspect which nervous reactions offer to the physiologist is the integrative …

Communication in the brain and the microchip

Communication between multi-input sources and multi-output destinations is a very complex process, done brilliantly but simply in the human brain from birth, for as long as 100 years or more. It is also achieved on microchips, but involves very complicated communication and mathematical techniques, all discovered within the past century.

For microchips, humans must pre-define a communication system comprising a transmitter, receiver, channel, distance, means of communication, and a signal.

The means of communication are wires on the microchip itself, as well as wireless off the microchip, as in smartphones. In both cases, the signal is an electrical one that carries a digital representation of the information.

This means that before transmission can take place, we must first encode the analog signal (speech, for example) via an A/D converter, taking into account the specific codes used, their ability to self-correct, the channel used, and the noise produced over the distance of communication. We can add encryption to the codes as well.

At the receiving end, we decode the signal and convert it to analog, again using speech as a familiar example. If that speech is used to search the internet for this book, however, an AI application (App) must be added into this process to interpret the information.

By now, you're getting an idea of the considerable design effort needed, the mathematical modeling, and the complex information theory behind the marvel that is your smartphone or tablet—even more so, that brain-mind marvel inside your skull!

A healthy human brain does all that with very little effort, energy, or power dissipation, which is all the more reason to take good care of your brain-mind and keep it healthy.

The future

There are two main challenges that the microchip industry must overcome. One is related to the massive physical expanse of their manufacturing and the second is concerned with the environmental impact of their production.

The first issue could be solved by using microscopic molecules rather than transistors as switches (copying the way the brain is designed) and using silicon in a 3D instead of 2D space, again copying the brain.

The second problem is more urgent in our time of climate change and resource exhaustion. This has been well-researched and addressed in *Making Microchips: Policy, Globalization, and Economic Restructuring in the Semiconductor Industry* by Jan Mazurek (MIT Press, 2003).

Nanotechnology

Advances in microchips are measured in their degree of miniaturization—more specifically, the ability to make tinier and tinier transistors. This in turn is measured as "the feature size." In 1990 Intel's 80386 microprocessor chip had a feature size of 1,000 nanometers, while Intel's Pentium 4 microprocessor chip in 2004 "broke the 100 nanometer barrier via the so-called 90 nm process," according to Philip Moriarty, Professor of Physics at the University of Nottingham, and author of *Nanotechnology: A Very Short Introduction* (Oxford University Press, 2022). "In December 2019," he continues, "Intel announced plans for 1.4 nm production by 2029."

Reverse engineering

As we have learned, microchips are micro-electronic circuits consisting of interconnected transistors and other semiconductor components. The microchip itself is covered by a layer of silicon oxide (glass) to protect the micro-electronic circuits underneath, both electrically and physically.

Counterfeiting microchip designs is accomplished through reverse engineering. This involves chemically removing the protective glass layer without harming the circuitry underneath. The next step is to examine the circuits and generate a net list. Once this is completed, counterfeit designs are possible, a crime referred to as IP (Intellectual Property) theft.

IP theft poses a great risk to the integrity and advancement of the industry, and no less so to the privacy of users. As a result, much effort has been invested in techniques to make the reverse engineering of microchips more difficult without significantly increasing their manufacturing cost. A recent report on deterrent techniques was published in the journal *IEEE Transaction on Very Large Scale Integration Systems* (May 2021) by Professor Emré Salman of Brooke University and his PhD student, Ivan Miketic.

For further reading

Ball, Philip. *The Elements: A Very Short Introduction*. Oxford University Press, 2002.
Blockley, David. *Engineering: A Very Short Introduction*. Oxford University Press, 2012.
Ceruzzi, Paul. *Computing: A Concise History*. MIT, 2012.

Cheng, Peter Lim Tze. *What I Learnt about Semicon and EMS: A Sharing of My Views on the Industry*. Tze, 2022.

Crandall, B.C., ed. *Nanotechnology*. MIT, 1996.

Elmasry, Mohamed I., ed. *VLSI Artificial Neural Networks*. Kluwer, 1994.

Goes, Sanket. *Microelectronics and Signal Processing: Advanced Concepts and Applications*. CRC, 2021.

Malone, Michael S. *The Intel Trinity: How Robert Noyce, Gordon Moore, and Andy Grove Built the World's Most Important Company*. HarperCollins, 2014.

Mazurek, Jan. *Making Microchips: Policy, Globalization, and Economic Restructuring in the Semiconductor Industry*. MIT, 2003.

Moriarty, Philip. *Nanotechnology: A Very Short Introduction*. Oxford University Press, 2022.

Pierce, John R. *An Introduction to Information Theory: Symbols, Signals and Noise*. Dover, 1980.

Soni, Jimmy and Goodman, Rob. *A Mind at Play: How Claude Shannon Invented the Information Age*. Simon & Schuster, 2017.

Swada, Doron. *The History of Computing: A Very Short Introduction*. Oxford University Press, 2022.

Intelligence— Artificial and real

I was finishing this chapter in May 2023, when international news media splashed the headline, "Godfather of AI warns that AI may figure out how to kill people."

For the past two decades I, along with the rest of the world, have been reading such sensational statements, including predictions that AI will make some jobs, and perhaps entire professions, obsolete. I didn't pay much attention; often the speakers didn't really know what AI can or can't do.

But the May 2023 headline, referring to Canadian AI pioneer and my colleague, Dr. Geoffrey Hinton, felt different. It was alarming, to say the least.

It was also strange—like Henry Ford (hypothetically) warning the early 20th-century public that using his cars could kill people. At the time, motorized vehicles were just beginning to replace horses and buggies and there was indeed genuine concern among the public. That concern turned out to be well-founded. After all, horses are sentient creatures with considerable brain-power; they rarely caused preventable accidents and certainly didn't "drive drunk," even if their operators did!

I am fortunate to know Dr. Hinton and his research work well, and referred to it some 30 years ago in my book: *VLSI Artificial Neural Networks Engineering* (Kluwer, 1994).

An Emeritus Professor of Computer Science at the University of Toronto, Dr. Hinton worked for Google from 2013 to 2023, resigning, according to media reports, "to be able to freely speak out about the risks of AI."

Before we proceed, however, it is important to know that:

1. Scientists and engineers *discover*—they don't "invent."

DOI: 10.1201/9781003486848-3

2. Humans kill humans—not the discoveries of scientists and engineers (personal firearms and nuclear weapons being iconic cases in point).
3. AI is short for Artificial (Machine) Intelligence—that is, a machine whose hardware and software systems are designed by humans; specifically microchip engineers, computer scientists, and computer engineers.

In an interview with CNN early in May 2023, Dr. Hinton warned that as a scientist, he "suddenly realized that these things (AI devices) are getting smarter than us." He went on to explain that AI could become a dangerously manipulative tool that can learn from, and potentially overtake, the intelligence of its human programmers. "There are few examples of intelligent things controlled by less intelligent things," he said.

In 1920, Karel Capek wrote a Science Fiction play called *Rossum's Universal Robots*, which ends with AI beings rising up against their human creators and taking over Earth.

The popular American SF author and biochemist Isaac Asimov (1920–1992) also expressed concerns about the power and potentialities of AI in his stories and public talks, long before the term became part of our daily language.

His controversial "Three Laws of Robotics," designed to safeguard against the AI dangers voiced by Dr. Hinton and others, was first introduced in his 1942 short story, "Runaround" (from the seminal 1950 collection *I, Robot*). Asimov's robotics laws state:

1. A robot (or AI machine) may not injure a human being or, through inaction, allow a human being to come to harm.
2. A robot must obey orders given to it by human beings, except where such orders would conflict with the First Law.
3. A robot must protect its own existence as long as such protection does not conflict with the First or Second Law.

There has been much speculative and scientific debate ever since as to whether Asimov's laws are even possible to implement; with the increased interest in AI, the discussion is once again very current.

As far back as 1818, Mary Shelley's powerful novel *Frankenstein: or The Modern Prometheus* introduced a memorable early SF scenario about the dangers of "creating" autonomous AI beings.

Capek, Asimov, and Shelley are among numerous SF writers over the past two centuries to have speculated on the concept of AI in myriad forms and contexts. Nearly always, the advantages are accompanied by dire predictions of unknowing or intentional misuse. So you see, fears of AI wiping out humanity are not at all new.

What is artificial intelligence?

But let's return to the most fundamental question of all. What, exactly, is AI?

As we mentioned earlier, AI is short for Artificial Intelligence, or more accurately, Artificial *Machine* Intelligence.

It refers to computer programs that perform certain tasks in place of humans, such as recognizing voices and faces—after a training process in which the program "learns" from examples, as well as from its mistakes. This is all done under the supervision of human experts in computer science and programming.

Theoretically, any task that can be defined, along with its measurable associated quantities, can be written as an algorithm and then turned into a computer program to execute that task with speed and accuracy.

Real-world fact

Theoretically, anything that can be defined, quantified, or measured, can be included in an algorithm that results in an AI App.

Such programs can be fine-tuned, using supervised learning from numerous examples and the guidance of specialized experts. For example, an AI program can be designed and written to recognize cancer cells in images of a patient's brain.

But here is both a problem and a paradox.

How do we define and measure *human* intelligence—its consciousness, reasoning, cognition, emotional expression, perception, prediction, creativity, and so much more that our brains and minds can do? Yet we humans *can* precisely define and program accurate spelling, diction, and grammar when designing an AI auto-correction program for text (although books, like this one, still benefit greatly from having human editors).

The ongoing uncertainties of "how" didn't stop H. G. Wells in his 1938 book *World Brain*, where he describes a global, self-aware AI. Based on a series of 1937 talks and essays, *World Brain* proposes the creation of an artificial, self-maintaining global "encyclopedia" whose information would be freely available to all people, regardless of race, culture, language, socioeconomic status, location, etc. Wells envisioned universal access to authoritative information as an effective tool for achieving world peace. Unfortunately, his vision did not materialize, although many would support the altruistic goals of Wikipedia as worthy of the effort.

For more than 5,000 years of recorded history, we know that humans have designed tools and machines to help them perform more and better physical labor to complement their physical power; and they still do.

For only the past 50 years, they have focused on designing machines to enhance and complement their mental labor; and they still do.

Our progress in AI development has been complemented by three major scientific advances in engineering and computer science—Artificial Neural Networks (ANNs), Machine Learning (ML), and Big Data.

AI surpasses human capabilities in being able to rapidly process huge amounts of information in order to carry out the tasks we program it to perform. At the same time, it can also receive and store similarly huge amounts of information to retrieve later.

When AI operates robots, it can perform tasks that would be dangerous or numbingly tedious for humans, such as detecting and clearing landmines, inspecting suspicious packages, doing endlessly repetitive product assemblies, or retrieving objects from hazardous environments.

When AI operates search engines in stationary devices such as computers, it can analyze and compare data that would take many human lifetimes to sort through, in order to almost instantly verify important information. Fans of the popular and informative Star Trek sequel series, *The Next Generation*, will recall how many times the amiable android Data performs vast calculations in a matter of micro-seconds in order to solve potentially fatal problems for the starship Enterprise and her crew.

RI—the real (human) intelligence

Now let us turn to the "real thing," human intelligence, or RI. What is it?

"Psychologists argued about it for most of the 20th century, and the debate continues," writes Ian J. Deary, Professor of Psychology at the University of Edinburgh in *Intelligence—A Very Short Introduction* (Oxford University Press, 2001).

Deary, who trained as a medical doctor and then practiced as a psychiatrist, conducts research and teaches about differences within human intelligence and personality, frequently within the context of medical disorders.

He asks: "Should we talk about human intelligence—human mental abilities—as one thing, or as many things: intelligence or intelligences? ... In psychology we tend to measure that which can be measured. Therefore, when we discuss the mental abilities and their relations, it must be kept in mind that, if there are some qualities that we value but we feel cannot easily be measured, then our account of intelligence will be limited. For example, we are relatively poor at measuring things like creativity and wisdom, some of the most valued human attributes."

Drs. Gillian Butler and Freda McManus in *Psychology: A Very Short Introduction* (Oxford University Press, 2014) echo the same dilemma, saying; "Despite being one of the most important concepts in psychology, intelligence is one of the most elusive to define ... Intelligence can simply be viewed as the ability to respond adaptively to one's environment, but this ability may involve many aspects—such as being able to think logically, rationally, and abstractly, as well as the ability to be creative and to learn, and to apply this learning in new situations."

They add that "Psychologists have questioned whether intelligence is a common thread underlying all mental processes (a general factor), or whether it reflects several different more or less related factors."

In "Recycling the Cycle of Perception: A Polemic," given at the 15th Conference of the Canadian Society for Computational Studies of Intelligence in Calgary AB, in May 2002 (edited by Robin Cohen and Bruce Spencer, Springer, 2002) Professor Alan Mackworth of the Department of Computer Science at University of British Columbia, writes:

"If we ask, what characterizes intelligence? We might answer with one, or more of the following nine views. An intelligent agent is:

1. Proactive: An agent achieves goals, implicit, or explicit. Its behavior is teleological, planned, and future-oriented.
2. Reactive: An agent perceives and reacts to environmental change. Its behavior is causal and post-determined.
3. Model-based: It uses models of the world to guide its perception and behavior.
4. Learning-oriented: It acquires new behaviors and new models.
5. Rational: It reasons, solves problems, and uses tools.

6. Social: It collaborates, cooperates, commits, and competes with other agents.
7. Linguistic: It communicates and coordinates using languages.
8. Situated: It is embedded or situated in a world to which it is coupled. It is particular, not universal.
9. Constraint-based: It satisfies and optimizes multiple external and internal constraints.

According to Dr. Mackworth's criteria, a computer program can be classed as an intelligent agent because it can make decisions or perform a service based on its environment, user input, and experiences.

Such programs can autonomously gather information on a regular schedule, or when prompted by the user in real-time. Intelligent agents may also be referred to as "bots," short for robots.

It has been more than three decades since Dr. Hubert L. Dreyfus (1929–2017), Professor of Philosophy at the University of California at Berkeley, published his classic book *Mind over Machine: The Power of Human Intuition and Expertise in the Era of the Computer* (Free Press, 1988).

He argues why the very idea of a machine being able to display human-like understanding is mistaken. Dreyfus reiterated his thesis in *What Computers Still Can't Do* (MIT Press, 1992), with *Still* italicized in the title for emphasis.

In his Preface, he cites Pascal's assertion that mathematicians who wish to treat matters of perception mathematically make themselves ridiculous, while the human mind "does it tacitly, and without technical rules." Blaise Pascal (1623–1662), one of the fathers of modern mathematics, was a French Catholic physicist, philosopher, inventor, and writer of the Age of Enlightenment.

Real-world fact

To date, scientists have created more than 10 definitions of human intelligence, or RI.

Moving forward

Two years before he turned 100, former American Secretary of State, Henry A. Kissinger (1923–2023) published *The Age of AI and our Human Future* (Little Brown, 2021). His co-authors were Eric Schmidt (b. 1955), who as

CEO of Google from 2001 to 2011 transformed the company from a Silicon Valley start-up to a global IT leader, and Dr. Daniel P. Huttenlocher (b. 1959), inaugural dean of MIT's Schwarzman College of Computing.

They write: "The AI revolution will occur more quickly than most humans expect. Unless we develop new concepts to explain, interpret, and organize its consequent transformation, we will be unprepared to navigate it or its implications. Morally, philosophically, psychologically, practically—in every way—we find ourselves on the precipice of a new epoch. We must draw on our deepest resources—reason, faith, tradition, and technology—to adapt our relationship with reality so it remains human."

On May 30, 2023, the American Center for AI Safety (ACIS) issued a one-line public statement saying, "Mitigating the risk of extinction from AI should be a global priority alongside other societal-scale risks such as pandemics and nuclear war." The statement was signed by 350 AI scientists and public figures, led by the above-mentioned Dr. Geoffrey Hinton. I (Mohamed Elmasry) was among the signatories.

In June 2023, the media reported that Sam Altman, CEO of OpenAI (the parent company of ChatGPT) U-turned on a promise that he would leave the European Union if it becomes too difficult for his company to comply with the upcoming EU laws, among them the requirement to reveal whose copyrighted material had been used in training AI systems to create texts, images, music, etc.

During the same month, serious talks between the United States, United Kingdom, and European Union were held to set up an international body overseeing the non-proliferation of AI systems, similar to the aims of the International Atomic Energy Agency (IAEA) in relation to nuclear weapons.

Lifestyle tip

Your RI is far more valuable than any number or combination of AI Apps. Take good care of it.

AI—the real story

But the real story of AI is a much older one.

In December 1943, just days before I (Elmasry) was born, Warren McCullock (1898–1969) and Walter Pitts (1923–1969) of the University of Illinois' Neuropsychiatric Institute, published a paper titled "A Logical Calculus of the Ideas Immanent in Nervous Activity," which proposed the advent of ANNs. With that paper, a new computer science field, Threshold Logic, came into being.

This was followed by Alan Turing's paper, "Computing Machinery and Intelligence" (*Mind*, New Series, Vol. 59, No. 236, Oct. 1950), proposing a test to evaluate whether "machine intelligence" could carry on a human-like conversation. It became famously known as The Turing Test.

The Dartmouth Conference of 1956 was the first technical gathering devoted to AI, then known under various names such as Expert Systems, Machine Intelligence, or ANNs, and is considered the official birth of the field within computer science. The following 20 years witnessed numerous breakthroughs in AI research.

In 1980 rules-based programs were introduced, and in 1986 Geoffrey Hinton, David E. Rummelhart, and Ronald J. Williams published "Learning Representations by Back-Propagating Errors" (*Nature*, Vol. 323, 1986), which allowed ANNs to do more things.

In 1997 IBM's Deep Blue defeated world chess champion Garry Kasparov (who had defeated Deep Blue only a year earlier).

In 2022 OpenAI released the still-controversial ChatGPT, an AI program using Natural Languages Processing (NLP).

Did you know?

Artificial Neural Networks (ANNs) are microchips that mimic the operation of neural networks in the human brain.

Hardware and software

Hardware is the technical term for any physical device that can compute, communicate, or do both, like the smartphone.

The first electronic hardware general-purpose computer was the 1943 ENIAC, a monster machine weighing 50 tons and using 18,000 vacuum tubes that were constantly burning out and needing replacement.

In 1981, less than four decades later, the first true "laptop" portable computers were made possible by the introduction of microprocessors—entire computers on a single microchip—beginning with the Intel 4004, developed in 1971.

By 1990, the accelerated pace of microchip development enabled the introduction of practical, compact mobile devices, including smartphones like the BlackBerry. Today, more than 85% of the world's population uses smartphones.

But during the early years, this was an entirely unexpected future. In discussions with my student Michael Lazaridis, co-founder of Research in Motion (which produced the world-famous BlackBerry), my thinking back then was; who wanted to be connected to the world anytime, anyplace? Perhaps only on-the-road salespeople, or truck drivers. We all had our eyes and minds opened very quickly over the ensuing decades, as the global popularity of smartphones exploded among *all* ages and professions!

Another historic Canadian case in which the future value of a new technology was vastly underestimated happened in the 1870s with the recently invented telephone, the smartphone's analog precursor.

George Stephen (Lord Mount Stephen, 1829–1921) went from very modest beginnings in his native Scotland to becoming a hugely successful businessman after immigrating to Canada at age 21. Twenty-five years later he was president of the Bank of Montreal. But he's best known for financing the coast-to-coast Canadian Pacific Railroad, which was completed in 1885.

Despite being a leading entrepreneur for decades, Stephen adamantly refused to own or use a telephone, even though the technology was available to him for nearly half his life and readily adopted by his equally affluent and influential business contemporaries. "He claimed the newfangled device was only used to spread gossip," writes Vivienne Smith in a 2005 British county journal, *Pioneers of Hertfordshire*.

Software is an intangible entity that usually takes the form of a computer program; literally, a set of instructions based on the *if-then* rule of logic. The first software was used in the 1943 ENIAC machine.

In 1965 a different type of software entered the scene, a rules-based computer program called Expert Systems. The development of this new approach to software progressed slowly and then stopped, due to the reluctance of human experts to articulate their hard-won expertise into software rules to which multiple users could have access.

But Expert Systems did help to facilitate the development of AI programs that "learn" through expert human guidance.

Did you know?

The original name for AI (Artificial Intelligence) was Expert System.

From preprogramming to apps

Microchips are the physical hardware of your smartphone. But before the smartphone is shipped to you, it must be preprogrammed by the manufacturer, otherwise its sophisticated hardware is useless.

Because they know exactly what kind of microchips have been built into each model, smartphone manufacturers can add compatible preprogrammed software to activate functions such as the phone's operating system (OS).

Once you receive your smartphone, you can personalize it with other software called Apps, short for application programs.

Apps must be compatible with your phone's hardware as well as with the preprogrammed software installed by the manufacturer—if not, your smartphone will not be "smart" anymore.

This is a very important concept to remember when we discuss the hardware and software systems of the human brain-mind, which are infinitely subtler and more complex.

The smartphone's OS is the program whose instructions manage all the other Apps that run on it. The OS follows an algorithm that tells it: first do this, then choose from the following actions, if certain conditions are met, etc.

Apps work similarly. For example, an App might be connected to a camera, a sensor that can take static or moving images; i.e. photos or videos. It can then store them and/or send copies to other smartphones or devices. Permanent or temporary storage of data can be on the smartphone itself, on a distant computer, on a memory device, or on massive remote servers called "clouds."

As the end-user of your smartphone, you have the freedom to delete photos, videos, messages and other data, or keep them. You can also use a variety of Apps to edit both text and imagery. And of course, you can share your stored materials with anyone you choose, or keep it completely private.

All of these options apply equally to material created by others, which you download and capture on your smartphone from social media platforms, websites, received messages, etc.

In the not-too-distant future, there will likely be smartphone Apps and sensors that can smell, feel, and taste.

Natural (human) languages and programmed (machine) languages

With the introduction of computers, special languages were needed to tell them what to do, but for decades these languages were important only to computer programmers.

The first such language was developed in 1883 by British innovators Ada Lovelace (daughter of the poet Byron) and Charles Babbage, who worked together on the Analytical Engine, a primitive mechanical computer.

From the mid-20th century, a number of languages emerged in quick succession, reflecting the rapid development of the computer age. Some of these included: Assembly Language (1949), Autocode (1952), FORTRAN (1957), COBOL (1959), Lisp (1959), BASIC (1964), Pascal (1970), C (1972), MATLAB (1978), C++ (1983), Python (1991), Visual Basic (1991), Java (1995), and many others, some of which are still used today. New programming languages continue to be developed on the concepts designed in older ones.

But several key questions keep arising. Can computers really understand human speech (Natural Language)? Can they correct spelling, grammar, and style errors (in other words, can they creatively edit)? Can they accurately translate both literal meanings and nuances from one language to another? Can they generate speech from text or text from speech?

A great deal of research effort has been channeled into answering these questions and has resulted in some remarkable successes, such as instant visual and aural closed captioning on social media videos or television programs, to make them more accessible to blind and deaf users.

But creatively-driven human skills such as writing original literature (poetry, plays, novels, etc.) remain difficult to achieve. You may be able to have an AI App write a speech or school essay, but its "life" experience will be limited in unpredictable ways and you could make a fool of yourself! Already, there are Apps being developed for professors to detect whether online documents (such as university student assignments) have been AI-generated.

However, one AI application that has been very successful since the mid-1970s, but hardly noticed by the public or mainstream media, is automated postal sorting systems that came in around the same time as regional postal codes. These machines can correctly decipher (and still do) a vast diversity of human handwriting from all over the world and then accurately channel millions of letters and parcels for efficient and correct delivery.

Other AI applications include online news and editorial content delivered to mobile devices, recruitment applications, personal assistance, security monitoring, market identification, customer service analysis, supply chain management, screening of social media posts for dangerous or offensive content, etc.

Algorithms

Algorithms are the steps taken by programs in order to do specific tasks. An algorithm can be executed by the simple analog means of pen and paper, or through the digital labyrinth of a supercomputer. Algorithms range from the very simple to the very complex. As their complexity increases, the number of choices for developing each step increases and the sciences involved in determining those choices become necessarily more varied.

The human RI and brain-mind also use algorithms. Discovering more about them is vitally important, but also very difficult. For example, reverse-engineering the intricate construction of the human brain-mind in order to better understand and treat the many kinds of trauma, mental illness and forms of dementia that attack it is a much more involved process than developing algorithms to program smartphones.

Consider the algorithm used to teach school children how to add two decimal numbers.

Step 1—Get ready.

Write the two given numbers one below the other:

0002.56700
2001.98089
Step 2—Do.

Add the numbers in columns from right to left, from lower to higher values. Add carryover digits, if any, to the next column on the left.

Step 3—When the addition is completed, go to Step 4.
Step 4—Review the resulting answer and correct any errors.
Step 5—When review/correction is done, go to Step 6.
Step 6—Hand over the result as per instructions.
Step 7—When done, declare DONE.
Step 8—Go back to Step 1.

The same eight-step algorithm can be used to write a computer program to run the calculator App on your smartphone!

The word "algorithm" is named after Muhammad ibn Musa al-Khwarizmi (c. 780–850 CE), an accomplished Persian mathematician who also contributed to the development of Algebra. His family name, Al-Khwarizmi, was Latinized to Algorismus, and then to Algorithm, referring to the steps taken to carry out a given task.

Let us now build an algorithm to preprogram the brain-mind of an unborn human fetus to know how to find and suck on its mother's nipple in order to be fed. It might go something like this:

1. Ignore the sense of sight (babies can see very little as newborns).
2. Select as input the sound of mother's voice and the touch of her hands to search for and find her nipple; then hold on!
3. Retain in memory the unique smell and taste of mother's milk.
4. Reject any other milk, unless you're starving.
5. Add the sense of sight when you can see.
6. Show pleasure when you see your mother.
7. Cry if you see a stranger's face, or when hungry.
8. When you are full, an involuntary sound will come from your stomach to your mouth; a burp, don't worry about it.
9. Save this algorithm in your brain-mind. Use whenever you feel hunger.
10. After about two years, you won't get any more mother's milk because there will be none left. Get used to it and don't fuss.

To duplicate such an algorithm and write a computer program for it would be next to impossible for an AI robot, but a newborn human does it with ease.

Closely related to the mathematical science of creating algorithms is the engineering of the architecture used to implement them, which must take into account the hardware that will execute the programming.

In the case of the human brain, complete details of its architecture are known only to its original Designer—whether you credit this to millennia of intelligent evolution, or to a supreme intelligent being called (for example) God.

The brain is an amazingly flexible and very sophisticated architecture that simultaneously executes myriad algorithms with high accuracy and speed, while using very little energy or power dissipation.

In the case of a computer or smartphone, the architecture is fully known to its human designers, but limited in flexibility. So the quest is always to develop increasingly innovative architectures.

In university engineering and computer science departments, we teach and do research on both algorithms and architectures, including ways in which they mimic those of the human brain-mind. Exploring both areas can help neuroscience researchers to reverse-engineer more and more functions of the brain.

Artificial Neural Networks (ANNs)

In order to imitate the amazing ability of the human brain-mind to self-learn and execute numerous simultaneous algorithms, engineers developed architectures called ANNs. I am one of those who contributed many technical papers to this exciting new field while teaching and researching at the University of Waterloo.

ANNs are not as familiar to the layperson as AI. However, ANNs are well known to both AI experts and microchip systems designers.

Engineers have long been fascinated by how efficiently and rapidly biological neural networks can perform such complex tasks as sensory recognition. Networks within the brain instantly recognize input from all of our five senses and perform a highly sophisticated integration of this complex information to make decisions and formulate responses, all with great speed, accuracy, and energy efficiency.

Theoretically, microchip (artificial machine) networks could be designed to perform similar tasks, such as recognition, but to exactly replicate human neural networks is impossible. Engineers turn to digital implementation as the closest alternative; first digitizing an image (for example), then processing the digital information using algorithms similar to those of the biological human neural network.

Although the switching time of biological neurons is a few milliseconds—or more than a million times *slower* than that of artificial circuits—the accuracy of the human system is always much higher.

The reason for greater accuracy in biological systems is their massive parallel connectivity and the fact that they operate in a 3D environment. At the present time, neither of these features can be duplicated in ANN microchips due to prohibitively high manufacturing costs, and the lack of massive research and design funding. But this could change in the future.

Machine learning (ML)

Our brains and minds are preprogrammed to know how to learn on many different levels—from others, from events, from external surroundings, or from observation and experience. We don't consciously know the sequence of steps required to learn something, but we do them all the time; sometimes quickly, sometimes slowly, sometimes imperfectly, sometimes with great ease and accuracy.

ML is the field of computer science concerned with writing programs that allow computers to "learn." Today, there are numerous applications that require ML techniques. Here are just a few examples:

- Smartphones that learn to recognize your unique voice patterns and distinguish your commands from those of others.
- Software that learns to extract useful and specific pieces of information from huge data sets.
- Anti-spam software that learns how to screen harmful or junk messages from your email.
- Anti-fraud software that can learn how to detect the unauthorized use of your credit cards or other private information.
- ML also has wide applications in medicine for screening patients' test results, scanned imagery, etc.

The computer science of ML examines fundamental questions such as: What is learning? How can a machine learn? Is true ML possible? How do we know when the learning is complete or successful? How do we know when learning has failed?

The story of ML began in 1958 when an IBM computer, weighing 5 tons and filling a big room, was fed punch cards. After 50 trials, the computer "taught itself" to distinguish cards punched on the left side from cards punched on the right. Frank Rosenblatt (1928–1971) a Professor of Neurobiology at Cornell, wrote the computer program and called his new algorithm a "perceptron." In its simplest definition, a perceptron imitates a biological neuron in an ANN.

"Stories about the creation of machines having human qualities have long been a fascinating province in the realm of science fiction," Rosenblatt wrote. "Yet we are about to witness the birth of such a machine—a machine capable of perceiving, recognizing, and identifying its surroundings without any human training or control."

Despite Dr. Rosenblatt's breakthrough algorithm, ML did not take hold in computer science graduate programs and research labs until the 1970s, when it encountered its close cousin, AI.

Up to this point, AI (which was still being called Expert Systems) was based on "if-then" programming rules, created with the help of field experts.

But the human experts experienced major difficulties when it came to translating their long years of knowledge and experience into simple if-then rules, so that software engineers could build them into useful AI programs such as (among many possible examples) how to recognize cancer cells among millions of healthy cells. Understandably, some refused to contribute to the programming efforts and AI was in danger of being dead on arrival.

So AI specialists decided to take a very different approach.

If it was too difficult to tell a computer what to do using if-then rules, why not teach the computer *itself* how to learn, using examples? It might take thousands or tens of thousands of attempts or examples until something could be "learned," but computers don't get tired, so they could be fed as many examples as needed.

With that radical change in programming strategy, ML as a bona fide computer science field was born. Its "birth certificate" was *Machine Learning: The AI Approach,* a thick anthology of research papers edited by Ryszard S. Michalski, Jaime G. Carbonell, and Tom M. Mitchell (Tioga, 1983).

In 1997, Mitchell published *Machine Learning* (McGraw Hill), which became a legendary textbook for ML graduate students. Thanks to the impetus of Mitchell and his colleagues, ML gained rapid momentum. Research conferences were held, new journals were established, and more computer scientists were drawn to ML as a leading-edge research field.

Today, many universities offer ML in undergraduate computer science programs, helped by introductory texts such as *An Introduction to Machine Learning for Undergraduates*, by Dr. Miroslav Kubat (Springer, 2015). The book was so successful that it went to a second edition in 2017.

Dr. Kubat is a Professor of Computer Engineering in the Department of Electrical and Computer Engineering at the University of Miami.

An Introduction to Machine Learning is written mainly for engineering students and is heavily mathematical, but Kubat discusses all concepts related to ML, with emphasis on those that have successfully achieved high accuracy, high speed, require little energy, and which dissipate low power.

In *Machine Learning*, Kubat writes, "the first thing to consider is bias: to be able to learn, the learner has to build on certain assumptions about the problem at hand, thus reducing the size of the search space. The next important point has to do with the observation that an increase in the size of the training set can actually hurt the learner's chances if most of the training examples belong only to one class. After this, we will discuss the question of how to deal with classes whose definitions tend to change with context or in time. The last part focuses on some more mundane aspects such as unknown attributes, the selection of the most useful sets of attributes, and the problem of multi-label examples."

Another excellent textbook is *Introduction to Machine Learning* 3rd ed. (MIT Press, 2014) by Dr. Ethem Alpaydin, Professor of Computer Science at Bogazici University, Istanbul.

And in the introduction to *Understanding Machine Learning* (Cambridge University Press, 2018), Shai Shalev-Shwartz of the Hebrew University and his co-author, my colleague Shai Ben-David of the University of Waterloo, write: "Machine Learning is one of the fastest growing areas of computer science, with far-reaching applications. The aim of this textbook is to introduce machine learning and the algorithmic paradigms it offers, in a principled way. The book provides an extensive theoretical account of the fundamental idea underlying machine learning and the mathematical derivations that transform those principles into practical algorithms ... We will discuss the computational complexity of learning, and the concepts of covexity and stability; important algorithmic paradigms including stochastic gradient descent, neural networks, structured output learning, and emerging theoretical concepts."

With all the effort and energy being invested in ML and the impressive results both achieved and promised, this is a good point in our journey to remember that the *human* brain-mind doesn't need any external programming technology to learn how to learn. If we allow it to do so through mental stimulation and cognitive exercise, it learns continuously on its own with surprisingly little effort. In fact, if we care for it well, our own brain can teach us a great deal about what it means to learn.

Lifestyle tip

Don't depend on AI to replace your RI, especially for tasks that require originality, creativity, imagination, or personal touches.

Big Data

Since the introduction of digitized information, Big Data has become its own subject area taught in universities; it's all about how to collect data, how to store it, how to analyze it, and how to use it. The fields of Mathematics, Computer Science, and Statistics have all contributed to the emergence of Big Data and its associated subjects, Data Mining and Data Cleaning.

But who has access to all this data? And what are the rules governing its use? Can we trust for-profit data collection companies? How about cyber security? Data encryption? Big Data studies are bringing all of these questions, and more, into much sharper focus.

Artificial General Intelligence (AGI)

The founders and developers of AI weren't aiming only for specialist AI systems but also aspired to create Artificial General Intelligence (AGI) systems with human-like capacities for vision, reasoning, language, etc. that could be integrated when appropriate.

In her excellent book *Artificial Intelligence* (Oxford University Press, A Very Short Introduction series, 2018) Dr. Margaret A. Boden (b. 1936), founding dean of the University of Sussex School of Cognitive and Computing Sciences, writes: "John McCarthy recognized AI's need for 'common sense' very early on. And he spoke on 'Generality in Artificial Intelligence' in both of his high-visibility Turing Award addresses, in 1971 and 1987—but he was complaining, not celebrating. Today (in 2018) his complaints aren't yet answered."

McCarthy (1927–2011) was among the founding fathers of AI; in fact, he coined the term itself while a computer science professor at Stanford.

Dr. Boden continues: "The 21st century is seeing a revival of interest in AGI, driven by recent increases in computer power. If that were achieved, AI systems could rely less on special-purpose programming tricks, benefitting instead from general powers of reasoning and perception-plus language, creativity, and emotions. However, that's easier said than done. General intelligence is still a major challenge, still highly elusive. AGI is the field's Holy Grail."

Close-up fact

Many more AI Apps are being (or have been) developed to do certain tasks and are waiting for regulators to allow their use.

The hybrid solution—incorporating AI in software systems

In some applications it's beneficial to use both learning and programming techniques in a given software system. Using only the latter can result in rigid and inflexible software, while using only learning techniques may be excessively time-consuming and not achieve good results.

The fruit-fly test

To highlight the huge challenges ahead in developing sophisticated AGI systems, let us examine the top 10 requirements for an AI robot in parallel with the capabilities of a fruit-fly, whose brain-mind operates successfully using only 100,000 neurons (human brains have more than 100 *billion* neurons):

1. The fruit-fly robot (FFBot) can take off, fly, and land with high precision. The angle of landing is varied and could be upside-down on a

ceiling. Takeoff is accomplished with no runway distance. Flights must be noiseless. Flying happens whether by night or by day. The autopilot works 24/7, with a life expectancy of 10 years.

2. The FFBot can be charged and retain its stored charge for at least 4 hours (a biological fruit-fly stores energy in tiny deposits of fat that are converted into sugar).
3. Hardware is light enough for flying at high speed while consuming minimum energy.
4. It can clone itself as needed, again using minimal energy.
5. It can use on-board software and smart sensors such as vision, hearing, and smell to recognize certain types of fruit. It can create a "sound picture" of its surroundings.
6. It can recognize "food-scams" (adulterated foods) such as vinegar.
7. It can navigate obstacles during flight and avoid traps, such as spider webs.
8. It can detect when its environment has become too harsh and go into sleep-mode, or a longer hibernation time.
9. Its multi-tasks through time-sharing of its hardware and software resources.
10. It communicates with similar FFBots.

At this junction in the history of research opportunities and funding for AI and its related fields, the big challenge will be to rescue this branch of computer science from the extremes of over-selling and fear-mongering. One can only hope that balance will prevail, along with progress.

The real difference between AI and RI

Alan Turing suggested that instead of trying to determine whether a computer could "think," we should determine whether a computer can make us *believe* it is thinking.

He posed the following test for skeptics and AI "converts" alike: If you ask a computer and humans the same questions and are unable to identify which source the responses came from then the computer is, to all intents and purposes "thinking," and the computer has "passed the 'Turing test'," says Professor Barbara Gail Montero in *Philosophy of Mind: A Very Short Introduction* (Oxford University Press, 2022).

Dr. Montero is Professor of Philosophy at the College of Staten Island and the Graduate Center of the City University of New York (CUNY).

She adds; "Most philosophy of mind discussions of the Turing test, however, do not concern the question of whether a computer could pass the test. Instead, parting company from Turning's original aim ... they concern whether passing the Turing test suffices for thought."

She concludes: "Passing the [Turing] test is *not* a necessary condition for thought. A very intelligent, thinking computer (or human) might be classified as non-human, because it appears to know too much or think too quickly. Of course, such an Intelligence might pass the test by dumbing itself down, yet it seems that one should not fail the test for performing too well. The concern, then, is whether passing the test suffices for intelligence." (Italics added.)

Star Trek's likeable android, Cmdr. Data, encountered this dilemma frequently on the iconic series spinoff, *The Next Generation*. In a number of episodes where officers from the starship Enterprise are required to disguise themselves when time-traveling, or investigating non-technological human societies, Data's astounding calculating abilities threaten to "blow their cover"—and sometimes did.

In research

The ways in which RI develops in the human brain from infancy, through adulthood to old age, have greatly influenced and inspired research in AI.

From Turing AI to a Darwin machine

While a Turing machine, programmed with AI software, is trained through iteration processes to learn and yield desired results, the software of a Darwin machine mimics the organic principles of natural selection, or evolution, in order to prune the results of its learning.

Real-word fact

While current AI can be misused to copy Shakespeare, write student essays, falsify Picasso paintings, and a wide range of other crimes or unethical purposes, effective AI Apps have also been developed to detect them.

But will AI take over?

"For 25 years I've begun my introductory psychology course by showing how our best AI still can't duplicate ordinary common sense. This year I was terrified that that part of the lecture would be obsolete because the examples I gave would be aced by GPT," confessed Dr. Steven Pinker, Professor of Psychology at Harvard in a *Harvard Gazette* interview of February 14, 2023.

"But I needn't have worried," he continued. "When I asked ChatGPT, 'If Mabel was alive at 9 a.m. and 5 p.m. was she alive at noon?' it responded, *'It was not specified whether Mabel was alive at noon. She's known to be alive at 9 and 5, but there's no information provided about her being alive at noon.'* So, it doesn't grasp basic facts of the world—like people live for continuous stretches of time and once you're dead you stay dead—because it has never come across a stretch of text that made that explicit. But to its credit, it did know that goldfish don't wear underpants." (Italics added.)

Pinker is the author of several books, including bestsellers *The Language Instinct* (Morrow, 1994) and *How the Mind Works* (Norton, 1997/2009).

In the *Harvard Gazette* interview he was referring to ChatGPT, the AI chatbot released in November 2022 by OpenAI. ChatGPT uses a Large Language Model (LLM) that enables it to continuously learn and improve its responses.

Pinker has pursued extensive research addressing links between the mind, language, and thought. Alvin Powell, the *Harvard Gazette* staff writer who interviewed Professor Pinker, said the purpose of his article was to determine "Whether we should be concerned about ChatGPT's potential to displace humans as writers and thinkers."

Pinker continues: "It's impressive how ChatGPT can generate plausible prose, relevant and well-structured, without any understanding of the world—without overt goals, explicitly represented facts, or the other things we might have thought were necessary to generate intelligent-sounding prose. And this appearance of competence makes its blunders all the more striking. It utters confident confabulations, such as that the U.S. has had four female presidents, including Luci Baines Johnson, 1973–1977."

"What we have now, and probably always will have," he concludes, "are devices that exceed humans in some challenges and not in others."

> **Future-proofing tip**
>
> Many of our future worries concern human jobs being taken over completely by AI. But remember, AI Apps are just computer programs, functioning as tools to help us increase the effectiveness of human jobs. Accounting and bookkeeping, for example, have been computerized for decades, but their programs have not replaced human accountants or bookkeepers—and they will never will.

For further reading

Aladdin, Ethem. *Introduction to Machine Learning*. 3rd ed. MIT, 2014.

Bach, Joscha. *Principles of Intelligence: PSI, an Architecture of Motivated Cognition*. Oxford University Press, 2009.

Baker, Muhammad Ali, et al., eds. *Agile Software Architecture*. Elsewhere, 2014.

Boden, Margaret. *Artificial Intelligence: A Very Short Introduction*. Oxford University Press, 2018.

Cohen, Robin and Bruce Spencer, eds. *Advances in Artificial Intelligence*. Springer, 2002.

Deary, Ian J. *Intelligence: A Very Short Introduction*. Oxford University Press, 2001.

Dreyfus, Hubert. *What Computers STILL Can't Do: A Critique of Artificial Reason*. MIT, 1992.

Dormehl, Luke. *Thinking Machines: The Quest for Artificial Intelligence and Where it's Taking Us Next*. Penguin, 2017.

Evans, Jonathan. *Thinking and Reasoning: A Very Short Introduction*. Oxford University Press, 2017.

Gross, Warren J. and Vincent C. Gaudet, eds. *Stochastic Computing: Techniques and Applications*. Springer, 2019.

Hawkins, Jeff. *On Intelligence*. St. Martin's, 2004.

Holmes, Dawn E. *Big Data: A Very Short Introduction*. Oxford University Press, 2017.

Ilyas, Ihab F. and Xu Chu. *Data Cleaning*. Association for Computing Machinery, 2019.

Jack, Belinda. *Reading: A Very Short Introduction*. Oxford University Press, 2019.

Kubat, Miroslav. *An Introduction to Machine Learning*. 2nd ed. Springer, 2000.

Louridas, Panos. *Algorithms*. MIT, 2020.

Medicine, John. *Artificial Intelligence for Business*. New Era, 2020.

Nachtigall, Werner. *Insects in Flight*. McGraw-Hill, 1968.

Pinker, Steven. *How the Mind Works*. Norton, 2009.

Shalev-Shwartz, Shai and Shai Ben-David. *Understanding Machine Learning: From Theory to Algorithms*. Cambridge University Press, 2018.

Sorin, Andrei. *Software and Mind: The Mechanistic Myth and Its Consequences*. Andsor, 2013.

Suleman, Mustafa and Michael Bhaskar. *The Coming Wave: Technology, Power, and the 21st Century's Greatest Dilemma*. Crown, 2023.

The brain-mind connection I

4

In this and the next chapter we explore the brain and its smart sensors, its interconnection and memory, its anatomy, and all the elements that hold it together. We then move up to a higher degree of complexity, to the human mind, Real Intelligence (RI), and how it differs from AI Apps. We consider the role of sleep, dreams, and humor—none of which AI can yet duplicate.

In May 2005, I was in London, United Kingdom spending my evenings watching live musical performances on the Strand and my days visiting old bookshops. In one of them, I bought a little book, only 79 pages long, published in 1950 and titled *The Physical Basis of Mind*.

The Preface drew me in immediately. I read: "This little book is a collection of talks originally delivered in the BBC Third Program, and subsequently printed in *The Listener*. The series was conceived and edited by a layman, one who has no claim to be a physician, a philosopher, or a scientist."

I was hooked! That evening, I skipped going to the Strand. With pen in hand I read and re-read every word, like a schoolboy getting ready for an exam.

The ten essayists of *The Physical Basis of Mind* included Dr. Edgar Douglas Adrian (1889–1977), 1932 Nobel laureate in Physiology and Professor of Physiology at Cambridge, who contributed "What Happens When We Think."

Two other notable figures were A. J. Ayer (1910–1989), Professor of Mind and Logic at University College, London, and Gilbert Ryle (1900–1976), Professor of Metaphysical Philosophy at Oxford.

DOI: 10.1201/9781003486848-4

The Introduction was by another Oxford professor and 1932 Nobel laureate in Physiology, Sir Charles Sherrington (1857–1952), considered the "Father of Neuroscience," who wrote:

> Knowledge of the physical basis of mind is making great strides in these days. Knowledge of the brain is growing, and our theme (in this book) is almost equivalent to the physiology of the brain. Mind, meaning by that thoughts, memories, feelings, reasoning, and so on, is difficult to bring into the class of physical things. Physiology, a natural science, tends to be silent about all outside the physical. And so the study of the physical basis of mind suffers from falling between two stools.

That modest little volume, *The Physical Basis of Mind*, published more than 70 years ago and purchased in a London used bookshop, inspired me to write, here in Waterloo in 2023, about the human brain-mind connection as an amazing hardware-software system—"all outside the physical" as Sherrington had put it.

The human body is often described as a system of systems. Each system, including our brain-mind, is perfectly designed and optimized to do its job with high precision and efficiency, within a small volume of space and weight using minimal energy, and can sustain itself through a life expectancy of some 100 years. To describe this natural phenomenon as an engineering miracle of the first order is almost an understatement.

More specifically, every system within the human body is actually a hardware-software system in its own right. Our physical biology, consisting of living cells that regularly die and are replaced, is the hardware.

Integrated within our biological hardware is our human software, whose basic operating system is preprogrammed before birth and automatically (involuntarily) upgraded as our bodies grow and mature. Humans are unique, however, in their ability to also upgrade their software systems voluntarily, as in the learning of new physical and cognitive skills.

Using a complex network of nerves, all of our body's integrated hardware and software systems report to the brain-mind, which serves as the headmaster or school principal.

Some of our biological hardware includes the skeletal, digestive, urinary, circulatory, respiratory, reproductive, nervous, immune, and endocrine systems. These systems are common to all human beings.

But the brain-mind system is very special, because its programming and content are unique to *you*, even though its basic physiology is common to everyone.

All of your other systems can be replaced wholly or in large part by machines, physical hardware (as in joint replacements), or through live transplants (such as human or animal organs and tissues).

Because our biological systems are made from trillions of living cells, most of which die and are regularly replaced, they are attached for life to their manufacturing source, the body.

This life-producing factory supplies energy to all the systems humans need in performing voluntary functions, such as thinking, talking, and walking, as well as involuntary actions, such as breathing, digestion, blood circulation, and, of course, producing new cells.

As David A. Bender, Emeritus Professor of Nutritional Biochemistry at University College, London, United Kingdom, notes: "Only about one-third of the average person's energy expenditure is for voluntary activity; two-thirds is required for maintenance of the body's functions, metabolic integrity, and homeostasis (maintenance of the normal state) of internal environment" (*Nutrition: A Very Short Introduction*, Oxford University Press, 2014).

The average total daily expenditure of human adults is about 2,000 kcal (calories and kilocalories are used interchangeably to represent the same amount of energy). That's enough total energy to heat 20 kg of water to the boiling point of 100°C.

> **Real-world fact**
>
> As a mobile and durable hardware-software system, the design of the human brain is an engineering miracle that can never be duplicated.

The kidneys

Let us explore one body system that can be understood at a purely physical level, the kidneys.

When human kidneys fail, they can be replaced physically with artificial kidney dialysis machines (usually considered a temporary solution), or for the long term, healthy donated kidneys.

The kidneys carry out two vital life-sustaining functions, both preprogrammed before birth. The first is to keep the volume and composition of body fluids more or less constant. By weight, water comprises about 65% of the body and is part of all its chemical processes, from digestion to the production of sperm. Without the kidneys, all those processes would rapidly slow down, and then stop.

The second function of the kidneys is to continuously filter and excrete wastes from our blood—especially urea, a compound formed in the liver by the breakdown of proteins. Each kidney contains a million tiny filters. And in both kidneys, 160 km of blood vessels deliver up to 2,000 L of filtered blood into the body every day, 24/7, whether we're awake or asleep.

The kidneys release liquid urine into the bladder where it's stored to be expelled. The bladder has volume and chemical sensors that alert us when it needs to be emptied. Most older children and adults are able to voluntarily empty their bladders at appropriate times and places, but there are a number of physical conditions that cause the expelling of urine to become involuntary.

Dialysis machines are artificial kidneys that can assist or wholly replace the functions of our kidneys, particularly the filtering out of toxic wastes.

Biology and physiology of the brain

While other vital organs such as the heart, lungs, kidneys, and even reproductive systems can be replaced physically or mechanically, our brain is a major exception.

Our physiological brain-mind contains our stored knowledge, memories, personality, creativity, and reasoning; in short, everything that is uniquely *us*.

And unlike the rest of the cells in our bodies, most brain cells do *not* regenerate if they die or are damaged.

Because the body is an interconnected and interdependent system of systems, the health or illness of any given system impacts the entire human organism.

Sir Wilfrid E. Le Gros Clark (1895–1971), Professor of Anatomy at Oxford, aptly defined his field as "the science of the form of living organisms." In the context of this book, anatomy deals with the brain's *structure*, while physiology deals with its *function*.

In *Human Anatomy, A Very Short Introduction* (Oxford University Press, 2015) Dr. Leslie Klenerman (1929–2015), Emeritus Professor of Orthopedic Surgery at the University of Liverpool, writes: "As shown most starkly by human stroke victims, the left side of our brain controls the right side of our body and vice versa … This arrangement serves no obvious function either anatomically or physiologically."

Dr. Klenerman adds: "Although the human brain accounts for only 2 percent of the body's weight, it receives 20 percent of the blood supply. In contrast, a chimpanzee's brain makes up less than 1 percent of its body weight and is supplied by a somewhat smaller fraction of its blood supply, probably 7–9 percent."

Another helpful resource for understanding the basics of brain anatomy and physiology is *The Brain, A Very Short Introduction* (Oxford University Press, 2005) by Dr. Michael O'Shea, Professor of Neuroscience at the University of Sussex.

"Any single neuron, out of the one hundred billion, is far too simple an entity to have any idea who you are," he writes. "However, conscious awareness of one's self comes from just that: neurons communicating with one another by a hundred trillion interconnections."

Dr. O'Shea adds: "Notwithstanding the brain's well-developed personal vanity, we must grant that it provides you with some very distinctive, abilities. It operates in the background of your every action, sensation, and thought. It allows you to reflect vividly on the past, to make informed judgments about the present, and to plan rational courses of action into the future. It endows you with the seemingly effortless ability to form pictures in your mind, to perceive music in noise, to dream, to dance, to fall in love, to cry, and laugh … Perhaps most remarkable of all, however, is the brain's ability to generate conscious awareness, which convinces you that you are free to choose what you will do next."

The nervous system

The brain communicates with our cells, muscles, and organs through nerve fibers, whose total length comes to some 500,000 km, or further than the distance between Earth and the Moon, which is only 384,400 km.

The brain sends hundreds of billions of signals or messages to our bodies every day, which is still more than the billions, even *trillions*, of messages sent daily by *all* of the world's communications media.

The human nervous system is divided into the central nervous system, consisting of the spinal cord and brain, and the peripheral nervous system which carries information back and forth from our sensory organs to the central nervous system in the form of electrical, chemical, or combined signal pulses.

In his classic book *The Integrative Action of the Nervous System* (Oxford University Press, 1906), Sir Charles Sherrington explains three methods used to study the nervous system.

The first is to focus on the nerve cells, which like all others in the body, "lead individual lives—they breathe, they assimilate, they dispense their own stores of energy ...; each is, in short, a living unit, with its nutrition more or less centred in itself. Here, then, problems of nutrition, regarding each nerve cell and regarding the nervous system as a whole, arise comparable with those presented by all other living cells."

The second approach is to understand how "nerve cells present a feature so characteristically developed in them as to be especially theirs. They have in exceptional measure the power to spatially transmit states of excitement generated within them via nerve impulses. Since this seems the eminent functional feature of nerve cells wherever they exist, its intimate nature is a problem co-extensive with the existence of nerve cells, and enters into the question regarding the specific reaction of the nervous system."

Sherrington's third method concerns the integrative, subjective action of the nervous system, which derives from its separate parts.

System biology

At each hierarchal level of a given system, its complexity increases correspondingly. This characteristic is studied in a new mathematical science called "system biology," which is well explained in *System Biology: A Very Short Introduction* (Oxford University Press, 2020), by Dr. Eberhard O. Voit, Professor of Biological Systems in the Department of Biomedical Engineering at the Georgia Institute of Technology.

He writes: "System biology is a new specialty area that actually has exactly the same goals and purposes as general biology, namely, to understand how life works. But in contrast to traditional biology, systems biology pursues these goals with a whole new arsenal of tools that come from mathematics, statistics, computing, and engineering, in addition to biology, biochemistry, and biophysics. System biology utilizes these tools to determine the specific roles of the different components that we find in living organisms ..."

The body, the beautiful

Every microchip designer knows that all of our human body systems, including the brain-mind, are ultimate in design. Moreover, beauty was also integrated into the design of every organ, inside and outside—an impossibility in microchip design.

"The body is one of the most beautiful and amazing machines in the world, filled with intricate devices, cunningly adjusted, wonderfully adopted," declared Dr. A. Y. Hill (1886–1977), 1922 Nobel laureate in Physiology or Medicine.

To appreciate the internal physical beauty of the human body through magnificent photography, I can highly recommend *Inside the Body: Fantastic Images from Beneath the Skin*, with foreword by Baroness Susan Greenfield (Firefly, 2007).

The human brain

The brain of an adult human weighs about 1.5 kg, or only 2% of average body weight. But it uses about 20% of the body's glucose-sugar energy supply and takes in some 50 cc of oxygen per minute. It contains more than 100 *billion* specialized cells, called neurons.

In fact, neurons are the primary cellular building-blocks of the brain, just as other groups of specialized cells form the rest of our vital organs.

The brain is also a very dense, tightly packed organ. Those 100 billion neurons function in a space whose 1,200 cc volume could hold just 18 medium-sized eggs. That translates to roughly 100 million neurons per cubic centimeter. Even today's most sophisticated miniaturized microchips have not achieved anything close to such density!

At birth, an infant's brain weighs only 350 g, or about 25% of its final adult mass. But it grows very rapidly. By the age of one, it has almost tripled to 900 g, and by age two, it has reached 1 kg.

The brain continues to grow throughout childhood and early adulthood. By age 25, our brain weighs in at about 1.4 kg and by 30 reaches its mature weight of 1.5 kg.

But by our 80s, the brain has gradually decreased in size down to 1150–1250 g, or a loss in mass of about 10%. Although we usually associate aging brains with diseases such as Alzheimer's and Parkinson's, it is quite possible to reach a healthy cognitive old age without developing any of the common neurodegenerative diseases.

The Brain Book (Firefly, 2012) by Dr. Kenneth Ashwell, Professor of Neurobiology at the University of New South Wales, Australia, provides a useful explanation of the brain's development, functions, disorders, and general health.

It's all in your head

The brain, the hardware component of the human brain-mind, is enclosed inside the skull where it has no direct contact with the external world. On its own, it cannot feel anything, not even pain; nor can it hear, see, smell, taste, or speak. It has no moving parts. It has no muscles.

The skull has proven to be the most effective protective structure for the brain. Like a custom-made helmet, it houses not only our most important organ but also its smart sensors for receiving information from the outside world and their complementary components such as nose, ears, and tongue.

By design, the skull is an engineering miracle in its own right. To maximize its toughness without a corresponding increase in weight, it is not (as many people think) an inverted bowl of solid bone; it actually consists of 22 bones, most of which are hollow or porous inside to increase their strength.

These bones are connected by joints called sutures. During infancy and youth, while the brain is still growing inside, the sutures remain somewhat flexible to allow for new bone growth, but by maturity, they have become rigid seams. The one important exception is the lower jaw, which is hinged at each side, but still considered part of the skull.

While the brain is tightly packed inside its protective skull, its enclosed environment remains comfortable, thanks to a surrounding envelope of cerebrospinal fluid that cushions it and the connected spinal cord against shocks.

These were the memories

The human brain-mind continually updates its memory banks every nanosecond, storing its acquired information in a non-volatile format (a space not subject to accidental deletion, under normal circumstances).

And the retrieval time for information stored in the brain's memory bank can be incredibly short, especially when responding to life-threatening circumstances, or in everyday activities such as speaking, or when simultaneously reading and understanding text or musical notation.

These human storage and retrieval capacities are far superior in design and performance than those of even the most advanced computers and smartphones. And it bears repeating that the brain-mind does all that with minimal energy uptake and power (heat) dissipation. Don't take it literally when someone complains that a challenging task is making their "brain burn"—it only feels that way!

Waking or sleeping, the brain-mind constantly processes huge amounts of information through multiple input ports, which include old information stored in its long-term memory, more recent information in short-term storage, signals from the body's internal smart sensors, and even more signals from its external environment, thanks to our familiar abilities to see, hear, touch, taste, and smell.

No matter what the task or situation, our brain-mind relies heavily on its stored long-term and short-term memories for all of its functions.

For example, when we "see," the lenses, retinas, and optic nerves of our eyes provide one source of input, but not the only one. To make sense, our physical seeing needs to activate relevant information stored in our brain-mind, and also be supplemented by accompanying input from our other senses. Thus seeing is a purely subjective human activity.

While monitoring and regulating all of our involuntary bodily functions, such as breathing, heart rate, blood pressure, temperature, digestion, and balance, our brain-mind is constantly making decisions without us ever being aware of them.

Real-world fact

Although housed in very close quarters within the skull, the human memory can store and retrieve enormous quantities of information, images, sounds, feelings, language skills, muscle memory, etc. throughout a lifetime that can last for as long as 100 years. It would take millions and millions of memory microchips, housed in a much larger space, to do even a fraction of all that.

If the average adult human's brain contains 100 billion neurons, it has even more neural interconnections wiring them all together—an unimaginable 100 *trillion*! And that's where memory really happens, in the connections rather than the neurons themselves. This is a design-engineering miracle that simply can't be duplicated in today's electronic devices; nevertheless, humans keep trying.

The serpentine folded and looped shape of the brain's external and interior structures allows maximum surface space within the relatively small container of the skull in which to pack its billions of neurons and trillions of connections, while still maintaining microscopically small spaces (called synapses) between them. While that makes sense as a design feature, it is still an engineering mystery as to why the brain is divided into two equal hemispheres.

The computational operation of each neuron is actually very simple: it switches on only when its input signals exceed a certain limit. This operation is asynchronous, meaning that neurons don't need any kind of timer or alert trigger in order to activate themselves.

Designing microchip circuits to operate asynchronously, however, is very difficult, especially for highly complex systems, so almost all microchip circuit designs are synchronized with a clock signal.

The number of inputs for each neuron is called the "fan-in number" and those for its output are called the "fan-out number." As we've just learned, both numbers are huge.

In our asynchronous brain system, neurons are active only when needed. But if the brain is damaged or diseased in some way and its neurons begin to activate synchronously, the mind and body go into seizure, as happens with epilepsy. If such conditions are not treated, the uncontrolled synchronized firing of large groups of neurons can cause the brain to lose its ability to manage and regulate involuntary functions, like breathing, temperature, heartbeat, and blood pressure, leading to death.

Even though the brain never takes "time off," its activity slows down and changes during sleep. Dreams that happen within the sleeping brain are much studied, yet still a profound mystery. What is the brain actually doing when it creates moving pictures with color and sound? Sometimes these images seem to have little or no relevance to our actual experiences.

It is thought by some sleep specialists and neurologists that dreaming allows the brain to refresh itself, sort out its memories, to "clean house" so to speak. Many studies have shown that people who are chronically sleep-deprived also dream very little and are more vulnerable to mental health disorders. Getting enough sleep is highly recommended for overall health, even though there is still much more to be discovered about the mysteries of the dreaming brain.

A boiled egg

We know by now that the human brain-mind is the most complex structure on planet Earth. But to look at it, it is not physically very impressive—it has the consistency of a soft-boiled egg, comes in a boring shade of gray, and is composed mainly of fat, the cushioning material that holds all those billions of neurons.

Yet as we've also discovered, it can live up to 100 years (sometimes even longer) with very little wear and tear, and without taking any time off. It is always on the job, receiving pain signals during physical or mental illness and injury to alert us that something is wrong. It also allows us to process information, reason, dream, and experience emotions ranging from love and pleasure, to despair and anger. It activates our muscles to flee or fight when we are threatened. It regulates all our body functions and stimulates the sexual responses and chemistry necessary for reproducing our own species.

One amazing capability of the human brain-mind that is far superior to even the most intelligent animals is learning.

Learning is much more than processing information for survival. It's about building a flexible, curious, and mature mind in which many skills are interwoven in unique ways that express creativity through our speech, song, dance, musical and literary compositions, visual and tactile arts, athletic prowess, research, inventions, discoveries, and so on.

Although humans have formalized their learning processes for millennia through organized schooling, most of what we learn right from infancy still happens in a free-flowing unsupervised way because our brains are naturally wired to do it.

Lifestyle tip

Your brain-mind is the highest-value asset you have, or will ever have. Increase its potential and longevity by caring for it early in life, keeping it and your body healthy, so it can continue to develop.

Smart sensors

Our smart sensors are also highly complicated systems, not only in their construction but also in how they communicate information to the brain-mind.

By definition, a "smart sensor" is a device that measures an input quantity and partially processes it, before sending the information to a central location. Our brain-mind centrally processes information received from all five senses, memorizes it, and acts upon it, without us ever being aware of it happening.

Just how the brain-mind manages to store and remember hundreds of thousands of images, sounds, voices, smells, tastes, and tactile feelings throughout our entire lives is not fully understood. In fact, we've barely scratched the surface—another engineering miracle.

Speaking of useful sensors, did you know that we humans have about 10 million smell receptors?

Although dogs have about a hundred times as many, our noses are still incredibly sensitive to some odors. We are programmed to find some smells particularly potent, such as those associated with sex. For millennia, humans have known that musk, obtained from the sex glands of certain species of deer, makes perfume more evocative and erotic.

Our sense of taste depends on 10,000 sensors in the mouth, most of them on the tongue. They are preprogrammed to distinguish among five main taste groups: sweet, sour, salty, bitter, and savory (or umami).

We taste sweet things at the tip of the tongue, sour things at the sides, salty things over the surface, and bitter things at the back. Umami (a Japanese term), however, can be sensed by the entire tongue and other mouth areas. Perhaps this is why it is one of the best-loved taste sensations in many Asian foods.

Each of the tongue's receptor areas is preprogrammed with different degrees of sensitivity. While we can detect sweetness at one part in 200, we can detect bitterness in as little as one part in 2 *million*; perhaps this was an evolutionary safeguard allowing us to detect poisons.

Although our sense of taste provides us with pleasure and enjoyment, it is much less acute than our sense of smell. It takes about 25,000 times *more* molecules of a substance to taste it than to smell it.

The ear is another of our essential sensory organs. It is a miniature biological receiver, audio amplifier, and signal processing system all in one. A healthy human can hear sounds ranging from 20 Hz (lowest pitch) to 20,000 Hz (highest).

Sound waves reach one ear a split second before the other, and at slightly different pressures. These minute but important variances allow the brain-mind to determine a sound's direction and origin. Next, our stored memories identify the character and desirability of that sound. Is it your mother's voice? The opening theme of Beethoven's Fifth Symphony? A fire alarm?

Our ears are so sensitive that it takes three types of audio speakers to duplicate their range—woofers for the lowest frequencies, sub-woofers for mid-range frequencies, and tweeters for the highest frequencies. And in addition to their impressive aural capabilities, our ears are also constructed with a precise inner network of fluid-filled semicircular canals that help us keep our sense of balance.

Vision is the most complex of all our senses. The amount of information our eyes collect and send to the brain-mind is vast, far more than most of us ever imagine. Our two forward-positioned eyes give us binocular vision, allowing us to instantly judge both distance and depth; when their signals reach the brain-mind, it processes them in 3D.

As the brain-mind processes vision information, it sends signals as needed to the body; these in turn cause us to act. When a person loses their sight, the brain-mind can compensate by "replaying" scenes and images from past experiences, often as clearly and accurately as if they happened yesterday.

For those born without sight, the brain-mind can "see" its external environment using the senses of hearing, touch, smell, and taste. No machine can truly replicate this amazing adaptability.

Humans rightly connect their sense of touch with the skin, a super-sensor that envelops the entire body.

But it isn't the outer layer of skin that senses how surfaces and temperatures feel. That outer layer is actually formed from overlapping layers of dead cells that are continually shed and replaced with cells from the living layers below. As skin cells move upward to become exposed to the air, they become filled with a fibrous protein called keratin, which is found in our hair and nails.

Below that protective keratin-filled outer layer, living cells pick up sensations that tell us if something is hard, soft, rough, smooth, hot, cold, and many other nuances of texture from our environment.

As Leslie Klenerman says in *Human Anatomy: A Very Short Introduction* (Oxford University Press, 2015): "The hand is a sense organ capable of transmitting to our brain information concerning the size, weight, texture, and temperature of the objects touched."

From just the brief descriptions you've read here, it's not surprising that human smart sensors are much better-designed and more efficient than the corresponding ones in our smartphones, whether you consider the camera (eye), speaker (speech system), microphone (ear), or the touch screen (skin).

And what about smell and taste? We are still a long, long way from inventing any devices that can emulate the efficiency and accuracy of what humans can do. As early as the 1950s, comedians and Science Fiction writers alike fantasized about a world with "smell-a-vision," but it's unlikely ever to happen.

Common sense

In humans the sense of sight provides about 80% of our knowledge of the external world. All global cultures have shared expressions equivalent to familiar English phrases such as: "seeing is believing" (I trust the evidence that my eyes give me); "I see" (I intellectually understand); "open your eyes" (be aware, pay attention); an "eye-witness" (seeing something important happen); or "a picture is worth more than a thousand words" (a picture contains details that are more quickly processed as images than as words).

We often hear others, or even entire organizations, framing their philosophy or business practices in terms of "having a vision," again invoking the eyes as iconic organs of truth. Throughout history, humans have learned to enhance and extend the capabilities of their physical sight by inventing telescopes, microscopes, cameras, etc. Sight and seeing, whether actual or imaginary, has always been a core value of human art—not only in pictures, paintings, sculpture, architecture, film, television, photography, etc. but also in the performing arts, such as dance and music, where seeing the artists adds to the sensory and emotional impact of their performance.

When speaking of the mind, we frequently learn through "hindsight," or our historical memories; and we often rely on them to plan future actions through "foresight," looking ahead with preparedness.

Freud noted that humans are visually motivated creatures who "see" even in imagination and dreams. When we engage in real-life pleasures such as hiking or camping in nature, in forests or by seashores, we often dream about these experiences in full color. For the same reasons, we often enjoy bird-watching, or growing gardens filled with blooms of myriad shades.

Sometimes, however, over-reliance on vision (whether physical or metaphorical) can distance us from our other senses, or from the viewpoints of other people. By focusing on a single idea, for example—what we often call "tunnel vision" or "blinkered vision"—we choose to alienate ourselves from other ways of mentally "seeing" alternative solutions to problems, or different understandings of life.

This is certainly not the case during our first few months outside our mother's womb. We need to use all our senses in very basic ways in order to survive and understand our environment.

As adults, we have tended to make vision our "intellectual" sense. It exclusively structures the universe for us "out there and in front," according to Professor J. Douglas Porteous, who writes: "It is important, but it's a cool, detached sense, and sight alone is insufficient for a true involvement of self with world. In sharp contrast, the non-visual worlds surround the sensor, even penetrate the body, and have far greater power to stir the emotions. These hot emotional senses are highly arousing, filling the self with feelings of pleasure, nostalgia, revulsion, and affection."

He adds that "smell, in particular, arouses emotions strongly and rapidly because olfactory signals plug directly into the brain's limbic system, the core of emotions and memory, crossing far fewer synapses than do signals emanating from other senses. Above all, smell and the other non-visual senses are deeply bound up with the experience of pleasure. The pleasures of food, love-making, and pets are impossible to imagine without the non-visual senses ... Thus smell, sound, touch, and taste are of vital importance for the achievement and maintenance of a person's sense of wellbeing."

Or to understand his multi-sensory approach in a very familiar phrase, we need to "wake up (eyes) and smell the coffee (nose)!"

Dr. Porteous is Professor of Geography at the University of Victoria, British Columbia, and author of several books and poetry collections, including *Landscapes of the Mind* (U of T Press, 1990).

Hearing can greatly enhance the appreciation of our surroundings. Sound is a multi-dimensional sense in that it functions both directionally and spherically, enveloping the hearer with magnitude and frequency. The reception of soundwaves by the brain through the ear often generates feelings of relaxation, recognition, memory, and emotion (widely ranging through sadness, fear, anger, joy, hope, anticipation, etc.); sound can literally change our mood in seconds.

Like hearing, our sense of smell also provides useful knowledge about our environment and is especially important for newborns. Through different odors, infants learn to tell what is good and what is harmful. As independent and adult humans, the sense of smell also enhances our appreciation of beauty in nature. And it's part of our sexual preprogramming, helping us to detect smells that are natural, real, and authentic.

Our skin, the organ of touch, is the largest smart sensor we have. The phrase "keep in touch" comes from our long history as beings who value physical contact for comfort and reassurance.

It can be argued that our sense of taste is the mouth's sense of touch, as our receptors for sweet, salty, bitter, savory, or combined flavors can alert us to substances that could be dangerous or even poisonous to eat. In all cultures, women seem to be more taste-sensitive than men, although scientific evidence is inconclusive. Metaphorically and esthetically speaking, however, women are often considered to have more "taste" than men in fashion, design, décor, etc.

Scientists have concluded that while it is possible for humans to function adequately with reduced levels (or even the absence) of one or more of the five basic senses of sight, hearing, smell, touch, and taste—Helen Keller (1880–1968), deaf and blind from infancy, is a celebrated case—we could not survive with at least some minimal remnant of sensory awareness with which to interact in our environment (Porteous, 1977).

Synesthesia

In his book *Synesthesia* (MIT Press, 2018), Richard E. Cytowic, Professor of Neurology at George Washington University and a pioneering researcher in the field, defines synesthesia as "the automatic conjoining of two or more senses."

"Indeed," he writes, "synesthesia may well be the basis and inspiration for much of human imagination and metaphor. The science of synesthesia now spans several levels of magnitude—from DNA at the molecular level, to early cognition, brain imaging, all the way up to whole-organism behavior that includes art and creativity."

He gives examples of how some humans have experienced synesthesia, such as identifying days of the week as having their own colors, or seeing letters, numerals, and punctuation marks as colored, even though they are printed in black.

And in the world of classical and popular music, synesthesia has long been known to give composers, and even some performers, a creative liminal edge, setting them apart from their peers.

Among the dozens of well-known musicians diagnosed or self-identified with this complex sensory condition, are Alexander Scriabin (1872–1915, Russia), Jean Sibelius (1865–1957, Finland), Olivier Messaien (1908–1992, France), György Ligeti (1923–2006, Transylvania), Franz Liszt (1811–1886, Hungary), George Gershwin (1898–1937, USA), Duke Ellington (1899–1974, USA), and Billy Joel (b. 1949, USA).

Dr. Cytowic further explains: "Synesthesia speaks to the essence of who one is. It celebrates the singularity of the subjective self. The emphasis on subjective, first-person experience matters because what critics always want is a third-person proof of it, a technical verification by some machine. I have always thought this sad because it betrays society's bias toward objectification. It devalues an individual's interior world and what is personally meaningful to them. Not everyone sees the world the same because each brain individually filters and distills the universe in its own unique way. Point-of-view turns out to matter a lot in both science and everyday life."

Dr. Cytowic is the also author of *The Man Who Tasted Shapes* (MIT Press, 2003), *Synesthesia: A Union of the Senses* (MIT Press, 2002), *The Neurological Side of Neuropsychology* (MIT Press, 1996), and, with David M. Eagleman, *Wednesday is Indigo Blue: Discovering the Brain of Synesthesia* (MIT Press, 2009).

Now you're talking

When the brain-mind sends communication signals to the vocal cords to instruct them to produce sounds or to talk, it follows a special algorithm.

The larynx at the back of our throats is the organ containing our vocal cords and is part of the respiratory system that includes our lungs and diaphragm.

When the vocal cords are relaxed during normal breathing, air passes soundlessly between them. But when the brain-mind sends them a particular kind of signal, they vibrate and make sounds. The tongue, teeth, palate, and lips refine those sounds from the vocal cords to form words, songs, the articulation of pitch on many musical instruments, or other expressive noises.

The body depends on the brain-mind as its central "headquarters" to manage both voluntary and involuntary actions.

This involves a massive physiological communications network where signals can travel back and forth as fast as 300 kph. But some localized responses are almost instantaneous, performed first and then reported back to the brain-mind later. The knee-jerk reflex is a classic example.

The brain-mind, along with our intricate nervous system, allows humans to do multiple tasks or actions in parallel. For example, a rock star can sing, dance, get cues from the backup guitarists, move around on the stage, change instruments, and wave to throngs of admirers. While all this is going on, the body continues to regulate breathing, heart rate, blood pressure, temperature, and digestion.

This intense complexity of tasks and functions, some voluntary and some not, are all managed through an asynchronous system, one that responds to both preprogrammed and programmed internal or external stimuli. Can we say once again that this is simply amazing?

What is wrong with you?

Fixing the physiological brain doesn't necessarily fix the mind; to believe that would be like saying that fixing a computer's hardware can also fix a problem caused by a virus in its software. Nevertheless, humans have tried this approach.

Portuguese neurologist Egas Monis (1874–1955) introduced the technique of psychosurgery (also called lobotomy) to cure or alleviate mental illness.

The process involved severing certain connections between the frontal lobe and the rest of the brain, destroying some brain tissue as well. The results were considered both questionable and controversial in later decades but were considered to be a breakthrough at the time. Monis was awarded a 1949 Nobel Prize for his efforts.

The brain-mind in history

About 4000 BCE, Egyptian researchers understood the lower level of the brain-mind as being the part responsible for walking and daily work, from attending to farm animals, to designing the pyramids, or ruling the country. They believed then that the brain and the skull containing it were one and the same.

They called the higher level of human consciousness—the part responsible for doing good in the world (or its opposite)—the soul. They thought that it, as well as one's morality, was located in the physical heart, not the brain.

For that reason, when an ancient Egyptian of status died and was mummified, the brain was discarded. But the heart was set aside in a jar with preserving liquid which would allow it to be examined and judged by the gods; and then, as they believed, it could be used again by the deceased person in the hereafter.

In his paper "Old and New Concepts of the Basis of Consciousness" delivered at the 1957 Anglo-American Symposium on The Brain and its Functions, Denis Williams quoted the ancient Greek historian Herodotus (c. 484–425 BCE) who gives a vivid account of the above process: "They first take a crooked piece of metal, and with it they draw out the brain through the nostrils, thus getting rid of a portion, while the skull is cleared of the rest by rinsing with drugs."

Dr. Williams continues: "This cavalier treatment ... reflects perhaps the indifferences of the Egyptians to the brain, an indifference which contrasts with reverence for the heart as the seat of the soul."

The concept of the heart containing the soul was carried over into the teachings of Judaism, Christianity, and Islam, with the crucial difference being that the heart and soul were understood to be in a *metaphorical* rather than physical relationship.

In his important paper, "Medieval and Renaissance Contributions to Knowledge of the Brain and its Functions" (also delivered at the 1957 Anglo-American Symposium on The Brain and its Functions) Dr. Walter Pagel noted that "In the third century BCE, the brain had been meticulously studied in the Alexandria school, notably by Herophilos (335–280 BCE), a Greek physician who spent most of his time in Alexandria and is often considered to be the father of anatomy, and Galen (129–216 CE) a Greek physician and philosopher. It was in the Alexandria school that the modern idea of basing medicine on anatomy and physiology was cultivated and so made possible a scientific medical system as Galen established."

Dr. Pagel adds: "In spite of the lack of neuro-anatomical knowledge, there is evident throughout the Hippocratic (460–370 BCE) Corpus the most lively appreciation that the brain is the center responsible for the control of the body. In his treatise *On the Sacred Disease* we read: 'Men ought to know that from the brain and from the brain only arise our pleasures, joys, laughter, and jests, as well as our sorrows, pains, griefs and tears. Through it, in particular, we think, see, hear and distinguish the ugly from the beautiful, the bad from the good, the pleasant from the unpleasant. It is the same thing which makes us mad and delirious, inspires us with inopportune mistakes, aimless anxieties, absent-mindedness, and acts that are contrary to habit'."

> **Did you know?**
>
> The debate about the connection between our physical brain, our reasoning mind and the realm of human spiritual experience beyond the physical has been going on for more than 5,000 years.

Dr. Wilder Penfield, MD (1891–1976), founder of the Montreal Neurological Institute in 1934 and one of the world's foremost neurologists, quoted Hippocrates as saying: "I assert that the brain is the interpreter of consciousness. Some people say that the heart is the organ with which we think, and feels pain and anxiety. But it is not so. I hold that the brain is the most powerful organ of the human body, for if it is healthy it is an interpreter to us of the phenomena caused by the air (oxygen), as it is the air that gives it intelligence. Eyes, ears, tongue, hands and feet act in accordance with the discernment of the brain."

Penfield further cites Hippocrates on epilepsy: "I am about to discuss the disease called 'sacred' but in my opinion it is not any more divine or more sacred than other diseases. It has a natural cause, and its supposed divine origin is due to men's inexperience, and to their wonder at its peculiar character."

Dr. Pagel notes that the Early Church Fathers—especially Augustine of Hippo (354–450 CE), Cassiodorus (490–c. 585 CE), Benedict (480–547 CE), and Isidore of Seville (c. 560–636 CE)—"were deeply concerned with the nature of the soul, its possible corporality, distribution throughout the body or concentration in certain places, its origin and its appearance in man. They could not avoid looking for information in the classical authors, as far as they possessed them, and with reference to whom they had to define their own Christian position."

The early Christian era was followed by the Golden Age of Islam (700–1400 CE), when a group of brilliant polymaths—men who were at the same time physicians, surgeons, biologists, psychologists, mathematicians, scientists, philosophers, poets, astronomers, Sufi masters, theologians, and statesmen—studied the human brain-mind and wrote volumes of reference books about their discoveries. Notable among them were Balakhi (850–934 CE), Avicenna (980–1037 CE), and Ibn al-Nafis (1213–1288 CE).

In his paper "Non-Western Concepts of Psychic Functions," Dr. Ilza Veith (1912–2013), Professor of the History of Medicine and Psychiatry at the University of California, San Francisco, reviewed the far-eastern concept that "… emphasizes the importance of numbers and numerical relations as expressions of an ordered cosmos: the belief in the soul that is only temporarily stationed in man's body, in the reincarnation of the soul according to its actions during its preceding periods of earthly life, and after reaching perfection (that it) would reunite with the World Soul."

Imaging technology

These are some of the current imaging technologies used to study human body structures, tissues, and brain functions. In research, some of these techniques are used in combination

Factual knowledge ("knowing that")

Angiogram: A special type of X-ray that produces imagery of blood vessels, including those in the head.

CT or Computed Tomography: X-ray images are digitally processed to produce 3D images.

EBT or Electron Beam Tomography: An electron beam is directed against tungsten targets that are put under the patient. The images are processed by a computer.

EEG or Electroencephalography: Electrodes attached to the patient's scalp detect regional changes in the brain's electrical activity. Its advantage is being able to follow electrical changes; its disadvantage is that its anatomical resolution is very poor.

EM or Electron Microscope: Instead of lenses to focus a beam of light, EMs use electromagnets to focus a beam of electrons in a vacuum, with magnification of up to one million times. This technology cannot be used on living tissue, however, because it cannot survive in a vacuum.

Endoscope: A miniature camera on a cable takes pictures inside the body.

FCI or Fundus Camera Image: This involves a specialized camera to photograph the rear area of the eye (called the fundus).

FMRI or Functional Magnetic Resonance Imaging: It produces an image of the brain in real-time during the performance of specific tasks.

GCS or Gamma Camera Scan: Also called Scintillation Camera, it is the imaging device most used in nuclear medicine. It simultaneously enables both dynamic and static images of the body to be recorded.

LM or Light Micrograph: A light microscope with magnification powers of up to 1,250 times.

Microphoto: A photo taken using a miniature lens.

MRI or Magnetic Resonance Imaging: The human body is placed in a magnetic field that excites atoms within the body causing them to emit signals that produce an image.

PET or Position Emission Tomography: Similar to CT, it traces a radioactive substance inserted into the body.

Resin Cast: Not used on living tissues.

SEM or Scanning Electron Microscope: An electron beam shines on a rotating object and the beam bouncing back from it creates a 3D image.

TEM or Transmission Electron Microscope: An electron beam is focused on a stained tissue and its image passing through the beam is recorded.

Thermogram: Produces infrared heat radiation images.

Ultrasound: High-frequency sound waves are used to record images.

X-ray: Electromagnetic radiation with wavelengths shorter than light penetrates tissues, forming an image on a photographic plate on the other side.

How microchips and AI can help the brain and the mind

Since the discovery of practical applications for electricity in the 17th century, the advent of electronics in the 19th century, and 20th and 21st-century advances in microchip design and AI (including features such as integration and miniaturization), our lives have been improved through the use of biomedical devices.

These devices can do everything from detecting brain tumors earlier than ever before, to allowing the dentist to make detailed panoramic photos of your teeth. There are even solid body parts, such as replacement joints being fashioned by 3D printers. And there is much more yet to come!

In research

New AI-aided imaging technologies are continually in development to assist medical professionals in patient pre-screening and ever-earlier diagnoses of serious diseases and conditions.

For further reading

Ashwell, Ken. *The Student's Anatomy of Exercise*. Barron's, 2012.

Buzsaki, Gyorgy. *The Brain from Inside Out*. Oxford University Press, 2019.

Cytowic, Richard E. *Synesthesia*. MIT, 2018.

Edward, Leon and Anum Khan. *Concussion: Traumatic Brain Injury, mTBI—The Ultimate TBI Rehabilitation Guide*. Edward, 2019.

Elliott, Clark. *The Ghost in My Brain: How a Concussion Stole My Life and How the New Science of Brain Plasticity Helped Me Get it Back*. Penguin, 2015.

Hill, Denis and Parr, Geoffrey, eds. *Electroencephalography: A Symposium on its Various Aspects*. Macdonald, 1950.

Klenerman, Leslie. *Human Anatomy: A Very Short Introduction*. Oxford University Press, 2015.

Porteous, J. Douglas. *Landscapes of the Mind: Worlds of Sense and Metaphor*. University of Toronto, 1990.

O'Shea, Michael. *The Brain: A Very Short Introduction*. Oxford University Press, 2005.

Ratey, John J. and Eric Hagerman. *SPARK: The Revolutionary New Science of Exercise and the Brain*. Little Brown, 2008.

Ratey, John J. *A User's Guide to the Brain: Perception, Attention, and the Four Theaters of the Brain*. Vintage, 2002.

Shilling, Chris. *The Body: A Very Short Introduction*. Oxford University Press, 2016.

Voit, Eberhard. *System Biology: A Very Short Introduction*. Oxford University Press, 2020.

The brain-mind connection II

Describing or defining how the human brain and mind are connected is difficult, to say the least, as this connection occurs over many different levels.

Mathematically, the connection between a given region of the brain as a physical organ and, for example, the thoughts, emotions, and behaviors it initiates, can be linear or non-linear. It can also be a square function, such as a cube or square root; or it can be an exponential, or step function.

Moreover, the brain-mind connection is also subjective; that is, qualitative rather than quantitative. It differs from one person to another, even between identical twins of the same gender, raised in the same household, and who live their entire lives in the same place.

A particularly beneficial way to examine how the brain-mind connection works is through studying languages. Humans use language to think and communicate. How effectively and fluently they perform these skills is an excellent measure of how their brain-mind connections operate.

As we've mentioned previously, human-engineered devices also use language. The highest level of machine languages is found in the programming used in computers and smartphones. Such languages are understood fully only by the programmers who develop and use them.

A high-level software language such as C, is not one that can be expressed verbally or in written form to be understood by humans but is used only by programmers to communicate instructions to a machine.

And for instructions to be understood and executed by a machine, the programming language must in turn be translated into a hardware language; that is, coded bits and bytes. At that low level of the language hierarchy, no human can understood the programming except through reverse engineering—a difficult process that involves one-to-many mapping (where

DOI: 10.1201/9781003486848-5

a code can be mapped back into different programs, but where only one is correct and intended).

The relationship between machine hardware and software languages is much lower in complexity and sophistication than human languages. In computers and smartphones, we call these the "natural languages."

The human brain-mind uses "natural language" to integrate high-level and low-level codes, allowing it to communicate with other humans in both written and verbal form. This is the way we express thoughts and emotions; how we discuss, describe, sing, recite; how we report events in the past and present; and how we imagine them in the future.

A unique feature of human natural languages is their ease of referring to time in every facet—past, present, or future. Machine languages don't possess this ability, nor do even the most sentient non-human communicators in the animal kingdom.

In his paper, "A Critical Survey of Our Conceptions as to the Origins of Languages," given at the 1957 Anglo-American Symposium on The Brain and its Functions in London UK, Dr. Macdonald Critchley (1900–1997) quoted Professor Max Muller (1823–1900) as saying that "human language is something more palpable than a fold of the brain or an angle of the skull. It admits of no cavilling. No process of natural selection will ever distil significant words out of the notes of birds or the cries of beasts."

Professor Critchley, a neurologist and then President of the World Federation of Neurology, published more than 200 research papers and 20 books. He further cites his precursor, Professor Muller: "However much the frontiers of the animal kingdom have pushed forward, so that at one time demarcation between animal and man seemed to depend on a mere fold in the brain, there is *one* (italicized in the original) barrier which no one has yet ventured to touch—the barrier of language. No race of animals has produced language."

Since then, however, there has been growing interest and research, especially among marine scientists, about whether the complex and ever-changing "songs" of whales, for example, do in fact constitute "language" that humans may one day be able to decode.

Another area in which the brain-mind connection has been very influential is in the treatment of mental illness and other neurological and psychological disorders.

During the Muslim Golden Age (700–1400 CE), physical brain health was treated through diet, particularly the use of special food supplements.

The mind was believed to contain three levels: the Nafis (closest to the physical brain), the Qal'b (within the physical heart), and the Soul. Physicians used dietary methods to treat the Nafis, while the Qal'b and Soul were treated therapeutically through personal and social intervention.

These treatments were documented in the writings of Balkhi (850–934 CE), Avicenna (980–1037 CE), and Ibn al-Nafis (1213–1288 CE). Drugs were rarely prescribed to mental health patients as a means of changing their behavior.

Today, many different drugs are prescribed, notes Dr. Matthew Cobb of the University of Manchester in *The Idea of The Brain* (Profile, 2021) in order to "increase the level of serotonin in the brain, therefore alleviating symptoms of depression."

Alternatively, noted Professor Ilza Veith (1912–2013) in his paper "Non-Western Concepts of Psychic Functions," also given at the 1957 Anglo-American Symposium on the Brain and its Functions "… the brain has always been completely ignored by Non-Western philosophers and physicians … The fundamental reason for the Far Eastern unawareness [concerning] the existence and the function of the brain is largely, though not entirely, attributable to almost complete lack of general anatomical information. It is also due to medical, religious and philosophical convictions which permitted the formation of specific theories of psychic function … In the orbit of Far Eastern thought the theories were derived from Chinese concepts on cosmogony and the resulting belief that man is composed of the same elements as the universe…"

Dr. Veith adds: "Often known by the US name of their most successful version, Prozac, the SSRIs (Selective Serotonin Re-uptake Inhibitors) have become widely prescribed around the world, and many patients consider that their lives have been transformed as a result. And yet our understanding of what happens when you take an SSRI remains virtually non-existent."

Dr. W. P. D. Wightman, Professor of History and Philosophy of Science at the University of Aberdeen says in his paper "Wars of Ideas in Neurological Science—from Willis to Bichat and from Locke to Condillac," (again from the 1957 Anglo-American Symposium on The Brain and its Functions), that "René Descartes (1596–1650), had indeed drawn on his knowledge of the strange effects on motion when the fumes of spirit or wine passed into the brain … The rather narrow connection of nerves and brain serves not only for separation of the subtle from the gross, the pure from the impure, but also in order that the most spirituous and subtle liquor, as it were distilled from the blood, may acquire a further perfection in the brain: for there it is aerated by a kind of fermentation, whereby it is further volatilized and rendered more fit to perform the office of motion and sensation."

Memory

As we know, both the human brain-mind and smartphone rely heavily on stored memories in order to function fully and effectively. But there are huge differences.

In the case of smartphones, their memories are physically well-defined hardware components that can be extended outside the machine using, for example, cloud computing platforms, or local hardware extensions such as external hard-drives, or hard-drive storage within non-portable computers. Up until now, this has not been the case for the human brain-mind.

Moreover, the memory's physical location in smartphones and other computing devices is easily accessible; it can be mapped into information and knowledge, and vice versa.

But human memory is by design a network, not a location. This network is distributed among billions of neurons. In fact, our cognitive neurons are implanted within a virtual sea of memory. In computer science terms, we call this networking phenomenon Logic in Memory Arrays (LMAs).

Human memory is also attached, again by design, to its own "dictionary" of meaning, called Associative Memory. That is, before saving new information, the mind attaches it to what it already knows and has previously saved. This allows less memory space to be occupied and is much more efficient than that of computers or smartphones.

Human memory can generate feelings of love, along with pleasure and appreciation for beauty, sadness, depression, anger, or anxiety. And for better or worse, human memories are very difficult to delete.

This is opposite to smartphone or computer memories, which reside in microchip locations, not distributed throughout the device. The user can pass those machine-stored memories through a filter to create nostalgia for sharing on a social memory platform. But the memories themselves cannot generate emotional feelings unless they are attached to a subjective lookup table.

Machine memories can also be deleted by the click of a button. While they can be retrieved within a fixed expiry date, they can just as easily be permanently lost.

The human brain-mind is so highly complex, however, that scientists cannot yet accurately map locations where different kinds of information are stored.

It may one day be possible to trace such mapping through the use of theoretical computer models. But the big challenge for science is the fact that human memories are by-products of our minds; they are a software phenomenon, not a physical (or hardware) facet of the brain.

This is evident from the fact that the number of neurons in our brains doesn't change much over the course of our entire lifetime, from infancy to old age, unless destroyed by Alzheimer's or other brain disorders, yet the memories held by this finite supply of neurons are immense and continually increasing.

The best way to keep your brain and its memory capacity healthy is to follow general guidelines for overall good health, physically, mentally, and spiritually. Having officially become an octogenarian in December 2023, this is what I'm doing right now:

1. Taking afternoon naps.
2. Not eating to excess.
3. Choosing healthy, minimally processed food.
4. Exercising daily.
5. Praying and/or meditating daily.
6. Reading and writing daily.
7. Traveling yearly.
8. Not smoking.
9. Not drinking.
10. Avoiding non-prescription drugs.
11. Not worrying.
12. Fasting intermittently. (I am a Muslim, so during Ramadan, I fast between dawn and sunset each day of that month, and occasionally, one or two days a week the rest of the year).

Lifestyle tips

Paying attention to our physical wellbeing has become far more widespread, but now we need to invest more in taking better care of our mental and spiritual wellbeing.

This is just my personal list; you can write one of your own. Perhaps one day I may add: *Remember to take the garbage out on Mondays!*

Human memories are active and continually changing, every second, 24/7. Because their information is stored throughout an interconnected neuron network, it is virtually impossible to isolate specific memory locations from each other.

This process of information storing is both holistic and involuntary. For example, we can remember the taste, smell, and texture of foods we have eaten; even when, where, and with whom we ate. Yet all of this occurs without us even being conscious of the process.

In smartphones we use involuntary memory functions when executing an App. Others become voluntary when we intentionally click "save," or just as easily click "delete." This is because a smartphone's operating system knows exactly where it saved that specific information.

This is not the case with the human brain-mind. Memories may exist within its neural network, but be temporarily or permanently inaccessible due to trauma. This is why it can be extremely difficult to recover from some kinds of physical or psychological brain injury.

Memory plays a major role in the learning process, both in the human brain-mind and in Apps used by our smart devices. Learning is scientifically categorized in four ways—unsupervised, supervised, reinforced, and associative. Memory itself has five categories—short-term, long-term, semantic, procedural, and implicit.

Our biological brain-mind system has no difficulty recognizing what kinds of learning and memory work best together; it does this with automatic ease. But the whole process is much more complicated when designing machines that can learn.

Because human memory is limited, it operates in the involuntary mode to conserve storage space and increase retrieval speed. We can override this mode by using intention as a motivator to remember a particular piece of information. For example, someone may say aloud, "I will never forget you."

Humans can also intentionally develop and test their memories by playing "brain games," or performing daily brain exercises. And when we are motivated to learn how to do something we like, at any age, we are also enhancing our memory capacity. By contrast, you can't exercise your smartphone's memory to make it last longer and/or encourage it to perform at a higher level.

To accustom the brain-mind to performing a specific act or skill, we must do it daily until it becomes familiar; ask any music student required to learn the scale of every major and minor key. Repetition is the most successful method to learn new languages, whether speaking them, reading them, or writing them. It also applies to reading musical staff notation, or other patterns in which symbols have very specific interpretations and actions associated with them.

Both short-term and long-term memories are used in these processes. Yet much of this skill acquisition, even when we feel very conscious and intentional about it (such as doing daily musical instrument practice) actually operates at a sub-conscious level—another way in which our brain-mind connections are truly amazing.

When we first learn how to read as children, we do it through supervised learning from parents or teachers. This involves engaging our "smart sensors" of sight and hearing. The eyes soon learn to move rapidly across the text, connecting pixels—we call them "letters" in everyday terms—and interpreting them as words. Then we convert the words into meanings that are part of our learned language.

So when you read a book, you understand that the physical object in your hands means "book" as well as understanding what the content on the printed pages of that particular book means. We also come to understand that individual words in different sentences can take on several meanings. The same intuitive processing happens for every "natural" or human language.

Again, language processing, interpretation, and text-to-speech conversion (or vice-versa) are almost effortlessly performed by the mature human brain. But writing an algorithm to enable a machine to do all that in multiple languages is extremely difficult. In fact, even the best algorithms fall far short of achieving the same accuracy and speed, using as little memory space, energy, and power wastage as the human brain-mind does routinely.

Real-world fact

While smart devices are getting smarter all the time, none of them comes close to duplicating the capacity, storage, longevity, energy efficiency, or self-healing capabilities of the original human brain-mind. With reasonable physical and spiritual care, this human software-hardware "device" can potentially last for 100 years.

Reconfigurable and modular

Two important features that help the brain-mind accurately perform so many individual and simultaneous tasks using so little space and energy, are that they are both *reconfigurable* and *modular*.

A good real-world analogy for this is a team of workers who can specialize not only in specific tasks but can also perform many other jobs in collaboration with their co-workers. They are directed by a manager that can sub-divide the team almost instantly into different groups whenever needed, in order to achieve the best results in the least time.

In computer science, the ability to change the organization of numerous interconnections is called *reconfigurable architecture* and the reassignment of task-groups is called *modularity*. Both are versatile and powerful features that represent huge advances in the field.

But the human brain-mind naturally uses reconfigurable architecture and modularity, 24/7. Its ability to continually reorganize its 100 billion neurons and their myriad interconnections was embedded in its architecture by the original algorithm Designer—an engineering miracle of the first order!

Real-world fact

The human mind comes with thousands of Apps preprogrammed before birth and adds tens of thousands more throughout its life. It would take millions of entire super-computers to duplicate our amazing organic software.

Mimicking the brain-mind in designing computer hardware-software systems with reconfigurable architecture and modularity presents some of the field's most interesting and difficult challenges.

Continued research in reconfigurable computing is important to overcome the trade-off between flexibility and performance in designing small mobile devices, especially smartphones. Reconfigurable architecture can adapt their hardware to run numerous applications in order to maximize performance. Two reconfiguration approaches are usually used— *fine-grained* and *coarse-grained*. When reconfiguration is used simultaneously in both hardware and software, it is called *co-design*.

"Modularity helps us to explain the process or practice of curiosity," write Perry Zurn and Dani S. Bassett in *Curious Minds: The Power of Connection* (MIT Press, 2022). "Evidence suggests that curiosity is supported by two circuits: the reward and motivation circuit, and the cognitive control circuit. The former is active during curious search and sampling, reflecting both motivation to obtain novel information and the feeling of reward when that novel information is obtained. The latter controls the timing and nature of both search and sampling, in part by monitoring whether cognitive resources should be maintained toward the current goal, or redirected toward other potential ones."

They add: "Neither circuit has a perfect one-to-one mapping onto the modules we just described. Instead, the two circuits span among those modules, indicating the existence of a coordinated—sometimes sequential, sometimes parallel—function, allowing us to engage in the complex process that is curiosity."

Interestingly, Zurn and Bassett are identical twins and are, respectively, Professor of Philosophy at American University and Professor of Bioengineering at the University of Pennsylvania. They have authored more than 300 scientific research articles in the fields of neuroscience, physics, network science, and complex systems science.

Does the mind have a structure?

Nineteenth-century scientists and psychologists believed that the human mind had only three major components—emotion, will, and cognition. But 20th century and later researchers found it to be a far more complex and nuanced web of relationships in which no single part of the mind operates alone.

"Just as in medicine where people may specialize in the functioning and pathology of specific organs within the body like the liver, the heart, or the brain, a parallel situation exists within psychology regarding the mind," writes Henry Plotkin (1940–2021) in *Evolution in Mind: An Introduction to Evolutionary Psychology* (Penguin, 1997).

Dr. Plotkin, who taught Psychology at University College, London, continues: "It must be emphasized that a structural description of a complex system doesn't imply a functional separation. For example, brains and cardiovascular systems are structurally separate components of our bodies.

But what happens in one can, and usually does, have an effect, sometimes a profound effect, on what happens in the other."

"Emotional states can and do have an impact on what we attend to, how well we are able to carry out complex tasks of motor co-ordination, and what kinds of decision we make when facing choices. Emotion, attention, motor control, and decision-making are quite different parts of our minds with separate neurological linkages, but functionally they are closely stretched together. The stretching, of course, is also a part of the structure."

In psychology and neuroscience, studying the structure of the mind is necessary to understanding human behavior "from the problem of aggression, through how best to teach our children, and on to diet, food choice and drug use, to mention just a very few; all are important issues in psychology."

Sleep

Sleep, especially afternoon naps or siestas that have long been a cultural staple among non-North American societies, seems to receive the least amount of scientific and medical attention as an important factor in maintaining good brain-mind health.

I am a good example of someone who regularly takes an afternoon nap, a habit that began when I was growing up in Cairo, Egypt, and later in Canada as a PhD student, researcher, and professor. Having just turned 80, I don't suffer from diabetes, high blood pressure, dementia, depression, or anxiety, as so many in my age group unfortunately do. I attribute much of that to the lifelong benefits of taking a regular afternoon nap.

To learn more about the health-giving properties of good sleep habits, I highly recommend *Sleep: A Very Short Introduction*, by Steven W. Lockley and Russell G. Foster (Oxford University Press, 2012). Lockley and Foster are neuroscientists at Harvard Medical School and Oxford University, respectively.

The introduction of 9-to-5 working days has been a negative culture shift in which "progress" has worked against the natural human day-and-night cycle.

Prior to the imposition of this rigid bracket of time, people would rise with the sun to start their workday and go to bed at sunset, all year around. Waking hours were divided into two active periods by a short nap, which actually enhanced productivity: both body and brain were able to rest and renew their energy.

An interesting and little-known fact about ancient and pre-industrial human cultures is that love-making happened mainly during nap times, which was natural to our mating instincts as a species.

Today, we are the only creatures who copulate during the dark hours of night, a time meant for complete rest. Thus we tax both our bodies and reproductive systems by breaking the ancient rhythms of evolution.

Sleep is necessary not only to make us feel better physically but also to actively recharge our brain-mind. A habit of getting sufficient sleep has been shown to increase creativity. Instead of staying up too late and pushing their bodies and brains to exhaustion, many scientists, engineers, artists, writers, and others have awakened from deep sleep in the middle of the night with some of their greatest ideas and contributions to humanity.

Sleep deprivation has the opposite effect, whether intentionally imposed or not. As experts in torture and interrogation know only too well, enforced sleep deprivation puts huge stress on both the brain-mind and body, to the point at which both will cease to function and can die or be permanently damaged.

In *Sleep: A Very Short Introduction*, Lockley and Foster emphasize how critically essential sleep is:

> For centuries, we have regarded sleep as a simple suspension of activity, a passive state of unconsciousness, and for centuries we have been wrong. This failure to understand the active nature of sleep is perhaps one of the reasons why our 24/7 society has developed such little regard for it. At best, many tolerate the fact that we need to sleep, and at worst we think of sleep as an illness that needs a cure. This attitude, held by so many in business, politics, industry, and even the health profession, is not only unsustainable but potentially dangerous.

Close-up fact

Along with good nutrition and regular exercise, research has found that napping is an equally important key to maintaining physical and mental wellness.

Dreaming

In ancient Egypt, dream interpretation was both an art and a science. In Genesis 37–50, the Judeo-Christian Old Testament tells of Joseph (the one of the many-colored coats), a one-time Hebrew slave who became a master of dream interpretation.

His accurate reading of the Pharaoh's dream about seven healthy and seven starving cows saved Egypt from a disastrous famine. Symbolism in dreams is often believed to be a foretelling of future events. And this is exactly what Joseph advised his ruler: for the next seven years, the Nile floods would generously saturate the soil with water and nutrients, causing abundant harvests far beyond the country's need.

But the following seven years would be stricken with severe drought and crops would fail. Therefore, Joseph advised the Pharaoh, for the next seven years Egyptians should build large storehouses for all the excess grain so the people would not starve during the predicted years of famine.

The Pharaoh took Joseph's advice and Egypt thrived despite the famine, while many of its neighbors did not. Even Joseph's own family members had to travel to Egypt to beg for food. Because the Pharaoh respected Joseph and his dream interpretations, he appointed the former Hebrew slave his Prime Minister.

J. Allan Hobson, one of the world's foremost experts on the science of dreaming, is Professor of Psychiatry at Harvard Medical School, whose research interests include the neurophysiological basis of the mind. He has authored or co-authored many books on the subject, such as: *Dreaming: A Very Short Introduction* (Oxford University Press, 2002), *Dreaming: An Introduction to the Sciences of Sleep* (Oxford University Press, 2002), *The Dream Drugstore* (MIT, 2001), *Dreaming as Delirium: How the Brain Goes out of its Mind* (MIT, 1999), *Consciousness* (Freeman, 1999), *Sleep* (Freeman, 1995), and *The Dreaming Brain* (Basic, 1988).

In much earlier times, Muhammad ibn Sirin (653–729 CE), a Muslim scholar from Basra in Iraq, collected dream interpretations from practitioners of his day and wrote them down in a 500-page Arabic *Dictionary of Dreams*. It was translated into English by Muhammad M. Al-Akili with a foreword by Mahmoud M. Ayoub, Professor of Islamic Studies in the Department of Religion at Temple University (Pearl, 1992).

Sleep researchers today are placing more and more scientific importance on dreaming as a necessary function of good brain-mind health.

Whether we remember them or not, dreams seem to be part of the brain's replenishing process, but can only occur after a certain amount of deep sleep. In our sleep-deprived western societies, lack of dreaming is increasingly being associated with chronic mental stress.

Several episodes of the early 1990s Star Trek series *The Next Generation* incorporated the emergence of medical interest in dreaming and mental health by building powerful plots around what happened when Captain Picard or members of the Enterprise's bridge crew became cognitively affected, due to dream-deprivation for prolonged periods of time.

Their reduced capacity to make sound leadership decisions threatened the safety of all. "Night Terrors" (1991), "Schisms" (1992), and "Frame of Mind" (1993) are among the best known for dealing with sleep and dream concepts that were controversial and newsworthy in their time.

Anesthesia

Anesthesia comes from the Greek word meaning "without sensation."

General anesthesia refers to a state of unconsciousness that is deliberately produced by the action of drugs on the patient. Local anesthesia refers to the numbness produced in parts of the body by the deliberate interruption of nerve function, usually without affecting consciousness.

"Under general anaesthesia the patient appears to be asleep," writes Aidan O'Donnell in his book *Anaesthesia: A Very Short Introduction* (Oxford University Press, 2012). "But general anaesthesia is not sleep ... General anaesthesia is considered to be a state induced by anaesthetic drugs (the patient cannot make it happen to him or herself), and one that is reversible, in the sense of not being permanent."

He continues: "The conscious mind is responsible for forming both experiences and memories of those experiences. If only one of those functions were interrupted, the mind might form experiences, such as pain, but not memories. General anaesthesia temporarily suspends the formation of both experiences (perceptions, awareness) and memories of those experiences."

Concussion

I am a devoted soccer fan. Every time a young player uses his (or her) head, I feel it in my own head. "Heading the ball" in soccer generates a substantial force of 50–100 G's on the skull that houses *you*. This can lead to injuries such as TBI (Traumatic Brain Injury) or concussion.

"TBI is a major cause of death and disability in the United States," says the website www.cdc.gov.

Falls are responsible for approximately 35% of brain injuries, followed by vehicle accidents at 17% and assaults at 10%; but the remaining 38% are caused by a wide range of contact sports, making them collectively most dangerous for the brain. Approximately 1.5 million people suffer TBI annually in the United States and 52,000 die as a result. The estimated annual economic cost of TBI treatment exceeds $48 *billion*.

Humor

For thousands of years, most cultures have found ways to express the popular maxim that "laughter is the best medicine."

The healing and restorative properties associated with the body's laughing reflex are well-known all over the world. Laughter enhances your intake of oxygen, stimulates the heart rate, balances blood pressure, and increases the release of endorphins (good mental health chemicals) by your brain.

The term Endorphin is derived from "endogenous" (within the body) and "morphine" (a pain-relieving compound). But endorphins are more than just natural pain relievers; they also put you in a positive state of mind. They ease symptoms of depression, stress, and anxiety, while also regulating your appetite and improving your self-image.

In addition to being triggered by laughter, endorphins are released during activities such as exercise, dancing, making music, getting a massage, eating, and sex. Interestingly, our brains can't store endorphins, but generate them on demand; the supply is immediately used up until the next occasion.

In his book *Humour, A Very Short Introduction* (Oxford University Press, 2014) Noel Carrol examines the relationship of humor to emotion, a jocular state of mind, and cognition.

He observes "that people are more likely to laugh out loud in a cinema with an audience than when they are watching the same film at home alone.

Indeed, we speak of 'infectious laughter'... Sometimes emotions can inaugurate mood states—mental attitudes which calibrate perception and memory to process everything under their aegis. When one is joyful, for example, everything takes on a happy cast."

Robert Provine, a behavioral neurobiologist at the University of Maryland, studied college students to find out exactly what made people laugh. After 1,200 "laugh episodes," he was convinced that most laughter has little to do with obvious jokes or funny stories.

In his excellent book, *A User's Guide to the Brain* (Random House, 2002), John Ratey, bestselling author and clinical professor of Psychiatry at Harvard Medical School, elaborates on Provine's findings. "Clearly, social context is important ... People laugh when they're nervous as well as when they are amused, and they may laugh cynically when disappointed." He adds: "In 1998 doctors at the University of California of Los Angeles reported that they were able to make a 16-year-old girl laugh by stimulating a tiny region in the left frontal lobe, the supplemental motor cortex."

For further reading

Al-Akili, Muhammad M. *Ibn Seerin's Dictionary of Dreams*. Pearl, 1982.

Butler, Gillian and Freda McManus. *Psychology: A Very Short Introduction*. Oxford University Press, 2014.

Butler, Gillian et al. *Managing Your Mind: The Mental Fitness Guide*. 3rd ed. Oxford University Press, 2018.

Braun, Stephen. *The Science of Happiness: Unlocking the Mysteries of Mood*. Wiley, 2000.

Clark, Wilfrid Le Gros. *Man-Apes or Ape-Men?* Holt Rinehart Winston, 1967.

Doidge, Norman. *The Brain's Way of Healing: Remarkable Discoveries and Recoveries from the Frontiers of Neuroplasticity*. Penguin, 2015.

Elias, Maurice J. et al. *Raising Emotionally Intelligent Teenagers: Guiding the Way for Compassionate, Committed, Courageous Adults*. Three Rivers, 2000.

Elliott, Clark. *The Ghost in My Brain: How a Concussion Stole my Life and How the New Science of Brain Plasticity Helped me Get it Back*. Penguin, 2015.

Foster, Jonathan. *Memory: A Very Short Introduction*. Oxford University Press, 2009.

Hobson, J. Allan. *Dreaming: A Very Short Introduction*. Oxford University Press, 2002.

Kolenda, Nick. *Methods of Persuasion: How to Use Psychology to Influence Human Behavior*. www.nickkolenda.com, 2013.

Livio, Mario. *Why? What Makes Us Curious*. Simon & Schuster, 2017.

Lockley, Steven W. and Russell Foster. *Sleep: A Very Short Introduction*. Oxford University Press, 2012.

Miller, Richard L. et al. *Psychedelic Medicine*. Park Street, 2017.

Nissan, Nils. *Understanding Beliefs*. MIT, 2014.

O'Donnell, Aidan. *Anaesthesia: A Very Short Introduction*. Oxford University Press, 2012.

Poynter, F.N.L. ed. *The History and Philosophy of Knowledge of the Brain and its Functions*. Blackwell, 1958.

Rose, Hilary and Steven Rose. *Genes, Cells and Brains: The Promethean Promises of the New Biology*. Verso, 2012.

Saxby, Lorie and Phyllis Hiebert. *Secrets from the Brain: Sharpen Your Thinking, Power Your Performance*. Working Brain Associates, 2010.

Sherrington, Charles Scott. *The Integrative Action of the Nervous System*. Scholar Select, 1907.

Torey, Zoltan. *The Conscious Mind*. MIT, 2014.

Zurn, Perry and Dani S. Bassett. *Curious Minds: The Power of Connection*. MIT, 2022.

6 Beyond the physical

Machines have no life "beyond the physical"—humans do.

Our distant ancestors designed machines some 5,000 years ago, even before the Egyptians built the pyramids, those iconic examples of ancient engineering achievement. Early human machines, or tools, helped people to calculate, communicate, travel, plan, learn, teach, produce food, do manual work, tend the sick, protect the elderly and newborn, and hunt.

Some of those machines helped humans to design better machines. Sadly, others were developed to maim and kill fellow human beings through crime and war. No other species does this!

To say that a machine is intelligent or can "think," insults all humans at worst and shortchanges our potential at best. Yet we turn to this distorting phrase often in our conversations and writing: it has been more interesting than fruitful.

We therefore shouldn't ignore things "beyond the physical" in dealing with human interactions. The term beyond the physical (BTP) is often confusing, however, as it has multiple definitions, multiple ways to measure it, and multiple ways of integrating it with our physical or biological systems.

In 1935, legendary theoretical physicist Albert Einstein (1879–1955) wrote in *The World as I See It* (Snowball, 2014): "Everything that the human race has done and thought is concerned with the satisfaction of felt needs and the assuagement of pain. One has to keep this constantly in mind if one wishes to understand spiritual movements."

DOI: 10.1201/9781003486848-6

Why beyond the physical?

In this book, I hope that exploring parallels between Real Intelligence (RI), the brain-mind, and smart Artificial Intelligence (AI)-based machines—such as human associative memory with its seemingly infinite database, and Very Large Scale Integrated (VLSI) hardware/software systems connected to cloud computing—will lead to beneficial advances in both areas.

This in itself is a strong argument for integrating BTP, under any name, into our lives.

By emphasizing the potential of BTP integration between human and machine processing, I also hope that major funding at both corporate and government levels the world over can be directed away from supporting war and arms production.

The interdisciplinary benefits of BTP integration could be enormous, especially for those suffering from numerous forms of cancer, mental illness, and neuro-degenerative conditions such as Alzheimer's disease, Parkinson's, and dementia.

I lost both a younger brother and a good friend to cancer, as well as a brother-in-law and other friends to Alzheimer's disease. In each case, I was an eye-witness to their pain, and that of their families, as they became deprived of their dignity and self-identity, condemned to wait until the end, as if on death row.

My daughter was recently diagnosed with breast cancer and my first reaction was disbelief. "She doesn't fit the pattern," I thought. She is a healthy young woman, a high achiever, an accomplished professional, an athlete (international-caliber marathon runner), eats a healthy diet, is an avid world traveler, and doesn't drink or smoke.

My family and friends have not been spared mental health challenges either and I have become acutely aware of the huge waiting lists for appropriate care all across Canada. Yet mental health patients here get much more attention than those in many other parts of the world, including my birth country of Egypt.

As the world slowly recovers from the unprecedented disruption (at least in modern history) of the COVID-19 epidemic, its aftershocks are all around us in the dramatic rise of mental health cases, especially among children and youth.

It is more relevant than ever to deepen our study of human and machine-based sensory and information processing. But in order to fully understand the parallels between them, we must also include evidence-based spirituality as an essential BTP component.

Ian McGilchrist (b. 1953), a prominent British psychiatrist, neuroscience researcher, philosopher, literary scholar, and TV documentary host, has authored three recent and seminal books on the human brain-mind connection—*The Master And His Emissary: The Divided Brain and the Making of the Western World* (Yale, 2010), *The Matter with Things: Our Brains, Our Delusions, and the Unmaking of the World*, Vol. 1: *The Ways to Truth* (Perspective, 2021), and *The Matter with Things: Our Brains, Our Delusions, and the Unmaking of the World*, Vol. 2: *What then is True?* (Perspective, 2021).

Throughout some 3,000 pages, Dr. McGilchrist argues: "If we are wreaking havoc on our ourselves and the world, and if our best intentions lead to paradoxical outcomes, it is because we have become mesmerized by mechanistic, reductionist ways of thinking, the product of a brain system which evolved not to help us to understand, but merely to manipulate the world: that of the left hemisphere. We have become blind to what the subtler, more intelligent and more perceptive right hemisphere sees. Consequently, we no longer seem to have the faintest idea who we are, what the world is, or how we relate to it. Indeed, there is a sense in which we no longer *live* in a world at all, but *exist* in a simulation of our own making." (Italics are in the original.)

As an author, and for you as readers, I hope that this book you now hold in your hands or are reading on a screen, can help pave the way to answering some of Dr. McGilchrist's fears and concerns by applying basic scientific facts to three key interdisciplinary topics—the brain-mind connection and RI; microchips, smartphones, and AI; and mindfulness-meditation practice.

Close-up fact

If it works—increasing your wellbeing, creating more happiness and benefit for you and others around you—it's good for you. This "golden rule" applies to all human cultures and societies.

BTP differentiates humans from machines

Several years ago my son, aged 47 at the time, had to undergo a major operation. Following surgery, doctors decided to put him into a medically induced coma. I was extremely worried, visiting every day and continually praying for him. It would be three months before he was able to talk to me.

I was pleasantly surprised, however, to learn that in addition to physical care, my son was receiving good mental and spiritual care as well. I don't know how many hospitals worldwide offer these "extras" to their patients, but I hope that all can provide them; if not today, in the near future.

Nearly 20 years ago, I wrote *Spiritual Fitness for Life: A Social Engineering Approach* (Pandora, 2004). I gifted copies of it to the hospital library, and the nurses, doctors, and supporting staff who took such good care of my son. Not long after, I decided to make it available free online at https://drelmasry. kotobee.com.

In that book, I draw parallels between spiritual and physical fitness, comparing more than ten different religious and belief traditions. I scientifically describe spiritual fitness (something rarely attempted), how to measure it, and its long-term benefits.

My son left the hospital five months after his surgery, a more spirituality fit person than before he went in.

Spirituality—why not?

The bad reputation given to religion by extremists and fanatics of all kinds (and sadly, *every* faith group has them) should not deter scientific research from going "beyond the physical" in studying RI and the human brain-mind connection and how it impacts our understanding of machines that may be incredibly "smart," but which have no spirituality.

In *Timeless Healing: The Power and Biology of Belief* (Fireside, 1997), Herbert Benson of Harvard Medical School cites a study of 92,000 people in Washington County MD, who went to church one or more times per week.

They were found to have had 50 percent fewer deaths from coronary heart disease and 53 percent fewer suicides than the general public. My case would be among them if I happened to live in that time and place.

Lifestyle tip

Exploring and nourishing your spirituality, no matter what your faith tradition, or even if you have no religious affiliation at all, pays off in increased wellbeing and wisdom.

All my life I have been intensely aware of my spirituality and it has helped me weather life's ups and downs. I am grateful that my peers think highly of my achievements as an internationally recognized expert in microchip research, design, and application. As a recent octogenarian, I am also grateful that my physical, mental, and spiritual health are above average.

I recall how my brother-in-law would drive his wife to church in Waterloo every Sunday and wait outside for her. When I asked him why he didn't go inside and worship with her, he answered, "I am not a sinner!"

In his classic, *Mystery of the Mind: A Critical Study of Consciousness and the Human Brain* (Princeton, 1975), world-renowned Canadian-American neurosurgeon Wilder Penfield (1891–1976) wrote: "Since a final conclusion in the field of our discussion (the brain-mind connection) is not likely to come before the youngest reader of this book dies, it behooves each one of us (scientists) to adopt for him (her)self a personal assumption—belief, religion—and a way of life without waiting for a final word from science on the nature of (the human) mind."

This statement is highly significant, as Dr. Penfield was not only a career neurosurgeon but also a renowned medical scientist who while practicing in Montreal made major contributions to the treatment of epilepsy by mapping various regions of the brain. He was also the first to operate on patients' brains while they were conscious.

Penfield established the Montreal Neurological Institute in 1934 and remained its director until his retirement in 1960. He further explains that: "In ordinary conversation, the 'mind' and 'the spirit' … are taken to be the same. Whether there is such a thing as communication between (humans) and God and whether energy can come to the mind of a (person) from an outside source after (their) death is for each individual to decide … Science has no such answers."

Elsewhere, he reiterated this fundamental mystery: "A century of scientific research has passed in mapping the different functions of the brain but none of them can explain the mind. (It) remains a mystery … *Possibly the scientist and the physician could add something by stepping outside the laboratory and the consulting room to reconsider these strangely gifted human beings about us. Where did the mind—call it the spirt if you like—come from? Who can say? It exists. The mind is attached to the action of certain mechanisms within the brain.*" (Italics added.)

Alister McGrath (b. 1953), Professor of Science and Religion at Oxford University, wrote an entire book on the subject of Dr. Penfield's comments—*The*

Big Question: Why We Can't Stop Talking about Science, Faith and God (St. Martin's, 2015).

McGrath, who has three PhDs—in Molecular Physics, Theology, and Letters in Intellectual History—asks if the need to believe in God (or another supreme creator/entity) and to search for meaning is hardwired into the human psyche.

As an internationally recognized scholar and teacher of theology-science connections, McGrath has authored many books, including the bestselling *The Dawkins Delusion? Atheist Fundamentalism and the Denial of the Divine* (IVP, 2007), written in response to Richard Dawkins' *The God Delusion* (Bantam, 2006).

> **Real-world fact**
>
> The behavioral and religious sciences are both evidence based; they are built on the same research and methodology foundations as biology, physics, chemistry, mathematics, and other empirical disciplines.

Spiritual intelligence

Long before the advent of AI, researchers studying various forms of human intelligence tried to define and develop tests for Emotional Intelligence. Now they have added Spiritual Intelligence to the list.

"I feel it has become crucial to get a handle on the notion of spiritual intelligence in contrast to other kinds and, in particular, Artificial Intelligence," writes Mark Vernon in *Spiritual Intelligence in Seven Steps* (IFF Books, 2022).

He continues: "The latest advances in the development of algorithms and networks have led experts increasingly to agree that the pressing problem for humanity is not that computers will become conscious. That may or may not have happened, depending upon whom you ask. The immediate concern is that AIs are already so pervasive that we are at risk of forgetting what it is to operate without their slick planning, cunning manipulation, and tremendous capacity for problem-solving."

Dr. Vernon is a British author, psychotherapist, former Anglican priest, and a member of the International Society for Science and Religion.

If we can be rightly aware of "what it means to be conscious of staying human" in the age of AI, he suggests, then we might flourish with it. He offers seven steps to reach that goal: knowing our story, discovering free-dom, seeing reality, reaching for the soul, learning to die, resonating with reality, and befriending the irruptions of sudden radical change.

Making up your mind—literally

Alister McGrath, cited above, explains that the mind decides "what is to be learned and recorded." The child grows and the mind comes to depend more and more on the memory and the automatic patterns of action stored away in the brain's computer. The mind conditions the brain. It programs the computer so that it can carry out an increasing number of routine per-formances. And so, as years pass, the mind has more and more free time to explore the world of intellect, its own and that of others.

"If one were to draw curves to show the excellence of human perfor-mance, those of the body and the brain would rise, each to its zenith, in the twenties or the thirties. In the forties, the curves would level off and begin to fall, for there are pathological processes, some peculiar to the body and to the brain that inevitably slow them down …"

"In contrast to the body and the brain later in life, the mind seems to move to its own fulfillment. As the mind arrives at clearer understanding and better balanced judgment, the other two are beginning to fail in strength and speed."

On May 20, 1940, C. G. Jung wrote to a friend: "Your destiny is the result of the collaboration between the conscious and the unconscious. The unconscious is useless without the human mind. It always seeks its collec-tive purposes and never your individual destiny… If you follow the river, you surely come to the sea finally."

Jung (1875–1961) was one of the world's greatest psychologists. The letter excerpted above is from *C. G. Jung on Nature, Technology & Modern Life: The Earth Has a Soul*, edited by Dr. Meredith Sabini (North Atlantic, 2002).

Meditation

In *The Science of Enlightenment: How Meditation Works* (Sounds True, 2016) Shinzen Young (b. 1944) states: "In every spiritual tradition, inner explorers have discovered that the liberated state is in fact a natural experi-ence, as real as the sensations you are having right now—and that through the investigation of your own thoughts, feelings, and perceptions you can awaken to clear insight and a happiness independent of conditions."

Young was trained in the three major Buddhist elements or schools of thought: Theravada (also known as Zen), Mahayana (or Bodhisattvayana), and Vipassana and was ordained in Japan in the Shingon tradition. A renowned teacher and researcher on meditation, he is widely in demand as a consultant, including studies conducted at Harvard Medical School, Carnegie Mellon University and the University of Vermont.

In *The Science of Enlightenment* he discusses topics such as neuroscience and the role of meditation, how mental illness can be treated with inner work, how to improve concentration, clarity, and equanimity, and how to experience the "wave" and "particle" of the self. In examining these and other topics, he draws on his extensive study of Christian and Jewish mysticism, shamanism, Buddhism, and Indian yoga.

Approaching the same questions in the Islamic Sufi tradition is *Psychology of Personality: Islamic Perspectives* (2022), edited by Amber Haque and Yasien Mohamed, with a foreword by Abdallah Rothman, Executive Director of the International Association of Islamic Psychology, which published this collection of 14 research papers by Western-educated psychologists.

Dr. Rothman notes: "There would seem to be a polarity between a model of personality that measures who we are based on materialist biological factors and a spiritual orientation that posits a soul that transcends biological determinants. However, the two do not have to be mutually exclusive. Indeed, Islam embraces both paradigms, a physical and spiritual reality of (the) human condition."

He adds: "From an Islamic perspective of personality, we do have innate tendencies that we come with when born into this world, which get manifested in DNA. And at the same time, we have the potential to transcend those tendencies and achieve a balanced personality based on the natural disposition of the human soul. Islam gives us a framework for understanding not only what we are meant to strive for in terms of the perfect personality, but a map of how the structure of the soul works in alignment with God's creation."

Lifestyle tip

Develop at least one hobby in which you feel engaged and passionate, the earlier the better. But it's never too late at any age.

Mindfulness

Mindfulness is fundamental to the practice of meditation. It's about being (or becoming) aware of yourself and your relationship to physical existence through breathing exercises, focused imagery, reciting special phrases or mantras, and adopting calming poses or postures. These and other techniques enable one to draw on mental and spiritual energy to overcome pain and stress, thus restoring wellbeing in both mind and body.

The term "mindfulness" originated in an 1881 translation of the Buddhist concept of Sati—the moment-to-moment awareness of present events—by Thomas William Rhys Davids (1843–1922), a British magistrate in Sri Lanka. Mindfulness practice didn't become popular in the West, however, until the 1970s. Since then, many books about it have become available. Courses and groups are offered nearly everywhere, and more recently one can participate via YouTube videos.

An example among many books is *Mindfulness for Health: A Practical Guide to Relieving Pain, Reducing Stress, and Restoring Wellbeing* (Piatkus, 2013) by Vidyamala Burch and Danny Penman with a foreword by Mark Williams, Director of the University of Oxford Mindfulness Center. It also includes a CD of guided meditation.

Williams is Emeritus Professor of Clinical Psychology and Honorary Research Fellow at Oxford's Department of Psychiatry and an ordained priest in the Church of England. His research includes psychological models for the treatment of depression and suicidal behavior. He developed the concept of Mindfulness-based Cognitive Therapy (MBCT) and is among the authors of *Mindfulness-Based Cognitive Therapy with People at Risk of Suicide* (Guilford, 2015).

He is also a co-writer of *The Mindful Way through Depression* (Barnes and Noble, 2007) and the second edition of *Mindfulness-Based Cognitive Therapy for Depression* (Guilford, 2012).

Most recently Mark Williams and Danny Penman authored *Deeper Mindfulness: The New Way to Rediscover Calm in a Chaotic World* (Balance, 2023), a companion to *The Mindful Way Workbook: An 8-Week Program to Free Yourself from Depression and Emotional Distress* (Guilford, 2014).

Also in 2023, Professor Williams received an honorary doctorate from the Faculty of Psychology and Educational Sciences at Katholieke Universiteit Leuven (Catholic University of Leuven) in Belgium.

Symbolism in the age of AI?

"The statement that symbolism is the most important thing in existence needs no apology," Martin Lings (1909–2005) asserted in his short classic *Symbol & Archetype* (Fons Vitae, 2005).

He goes on to explain: "If Symbolism is deeply understood, it has been known to change altogether a (person's) life; and it could indeed be said that most of the problems of the modern world result from ignorance of the meaning of Symbolism. There is no traditional spirituality which doesn't teach that this world is the world of symbols, inasmuch as it contains nothing which is not a symbol. A (person) should therefore understand at least what that means, not only because he (or she) has to live in the here below, but also above all because without such understanding he (or she) would fail to understand (themselves) … being the supreme and central symbol in the terrestrial state."

Lings was an English Sufi Master, philosopher, scholar, and author of some 20 books, including the important reference biography, *Muhammad: His Life Based on the Earliest Sources* (Islamic Texts Society, 1983) as well as *The Qur'anic Art of Calligraphy* (World of Islam Trust, 1976). The latter book is distinguished with a foreword by the former HRH Charles, Prince of Wales, who in 2022 became King Charles III.

The leading German philosopher Arthur Schopenhauer (1788–1860) explains in *The Wisdom of Life* (trans. T. Bailey Saunders, Dover, 2004): "If a (person) finds him (or her)self in possession of great mental functions, (they) should venture on the solution of the hardest of all problems; those which concern nature as a whole and humanity in its widest range, extending (their) views equally in all directions without ever straying too far amid the intricacies of various by-paths, or invading regions little known; in other words, without occupying (themselves) with special branches of knowledge.

"The common objects of life will give (one) material for new theories, at once serious and true. The service he (or she) renders will be appreciated by all those—and they form a great part of humankind—who know the facts … What a vast distinction there is between students of physics, chemistry, anatomy, mineralogy, zoology, philology, history, and (those) who deal with the great facts of human life, the poet and the philosopher."

John Hick (1922–2012), Professor of the Philosophy of Religion at the University of Birmingham, authored many influential books including *The New Frontier of Religion and Science, Religious Experience, Neuroscience* and the Transcendent (Palgrave, 2006), An Interpretation of Religion (Yale, 1989 and 2004) and Disputed Questions in Theology and the Philosophy of Religion (Yale, 1993).

Dr. Hick observes: "I attended frequently Jewish synagogues, Muslim mosques, Sikh gurdwaras and Hindu temples, as well as Christian churches. And in all these places of worship I soon realized something that is obvious enough once noticed, yet momentous in its implications. This is that although the language and the liturgical actions and the culture ethos differ greatly in each case, yet from a religious point of view basically the same thing is going on, namely, human beings are coming together within the framework of an ancient and highly developed tradition to open their hearts and minds to God, whom they believe to make a total claim upon the living of their lives, demanding of them, in the words of one of the prophets, 'to do justice, and to love kindness, and to walk humbly with your God' (Micah 6:8)."

Darwin and beyond the physical

Evə'luːʃn Evolution: the gradual development of something, from a simple to a more complex form.

Revəluːʃən Revolution: a successful attempt by a large group of people to change a system—when evolutionary development seems to be happening too fast.

In speaking of smartphones, they are often described as "evolving" from one generation to the next; 4G, to 5G, to 6G and maybe to 10G and beyond.

But when we speak of digital microchips—my area of expertise for the past half-century—their technology is more often described as "revolutionary."

Because of vast public media advertising and their presence in nearly everyone's hand or pocket, ever-evolving smartphones are acknowledged by the general public. But the 1960s revolution in digital microchips and Moore's Law—which predicted their rapid doubling of capacity in ever-shorter intervals of time—are mainly known only to experts in the field.

This closely related evolution and revolution has been possible only through the cumulative research efforts of thousands of expert scientists and engineers. Some have been recognized by prestigious honors such as the Nobel Prize, but most remain relatively unknown except among their own colleagues and peers.

This is certainly the case with the grandest system design of them all—the Universe. Our planet Earth, including everything on it and in it, has gone through nearly 14 billion years of evolution *and* revolution, following laws set up at an infinitely distant beginning by its supreme Designer.

From the time when they first became self-sentient beings, humans have asked: Who made everything? Who made us? And *why*? As they evolved, they created many kinds of origin stories and kept trying to find answers about what was/is behind it all. Eventually, they decided that the Designer of Everything must be absolutely and infinitely knowledgeable and could only be *one* entity. And that Entity would have to be so omnipotent as to transcend the physical, the design itself.

In explaining his theories of evolution to the world, Charles Darwin (1809–1882) was talking about the design, not the designer. Similarly, the later "Big Bang" cosmologists were also talking about the universe's initial design, not the designer. And when it came to the microchip revolution, the famous Moore's Law of capacity growth addressed future microchip designs, not the designers.

Darwin's Theory of Evolution, first proposed in 1859, became well known even to school children. But equally (and perhaps more) important is the much less familiar Rudolf Virchow (1821–1902). Virchow, a Polish-German pathologist, physician, and statesman, discovered conclusively that every plant and animal is made up of tissues and every tissue is made up of cells. In his 1858 book, *Cellular Pathology*, he was the first to prove that "every cell must come from a cell."

Chandler M. Brooks, Professor of Physiology at the State University of New York, gave central credit to Virchow's work in his 1957 paper, *Current Development in Thought and the Past Evolution of Ideas Concerning Integrative Function*.

As we have seen, Moore's Law is based on the observation that the number of transistors on a microchip doubles about every two years, but it's more the observation of a trend rather than a law of physics. Gordon Moore (1929–2023) was a scientist and co-founder of the giant microchip manufacturer, Intel.

Does Moore's Law have an upper limit? Its originator would never say and experts disagree on when the law might cease to apply. One thing we know for sure is that over the past decade (2013–2023) the rate of increase for the number of transistors on a microchip is slowing down. Moore's Law has been useful, however, in pushing researchers to find a material other than silicon with which to design and fabricate microchips.

Again, Darwin is better known to the general public than Moore. This is because he developed a theory to explain his observations about the vast diversity of all living things. Darwin was another observer who didn't talk about a designer, only the results.

Moreover, neither Darwin nor Moore told the entire story—and they didn't intend to.

Darwin's Theory of Evolution is useful in understanding the constant transformation or mutation of bacteria and viruses and in developing effective ways to protect ourselves against the diseases they cause.

Here are some interesting comparisons:

- While the time scale of Moore's Law is in years (or, perhaps, decades), that of Darwin's theory is in *billions* of years.
- Moore's Law was designed by an expert with around 50 years of experience; the Designer behind Darwin's evolutionary theory is one of infinite, timeless experience.
- The designer of Moore's Law knew the work of previous designers very well; the Designer who inspired Darwin is the first and only designer of *everything*.
- The designer of Moore's Law had to follow pre-existing laws of physics and chemistry; the Designer behind Darwin's theory created all those pre-existing laws from nothing, from *absolute zero*.

In his book, *Am I A Monkey? Six Big Questions about Evolution* (Johns Hopkins, 2010), Francisco J. Ayala, Professor of Biological Sciences, Ecology, and Evolutionary Biology and Professor of Logic and the Philosophy of Science at the University of California, Irvine, writes: "The proper relationship between science and religion can, for people of faith, be mutually motivating and inspiring. Science may inspire religious beliefs and religious behavior, as we respond with awe to the immensity of the universe, the glorious diversity and wondrous adaptation of organisms, and the marvels of the human brain and the human mind."

Ayala continues: "Religion promotes reverence for creation, for humankind as well as for the world of life and the environment. For scientists and others, religion is often a motivating force and source of inspiration for investigating the marvelous world of the creation and solving the puzzles with which it confronts us."

And if there is any doubt as to where Charles Darwin himself stood, one has only to turn to his *The Origin of Species* (1859) where he marveled that *"There is grandeur in this view of life, with its several powers, having been originally breathed by the Creator into a few forms or one form."* (Italics added.)

Lifestyle tip

In our age of overwhelming free online information, take the time to seek out a few authoritative resources when you want authentic knowledge.

Complexity system theory

"A complex system is a system formed out of many components whose behavior is emergent, that is, cannot be simply inferred from the behavior of its components. The amount of information necessary to describe the behavior of such a system is a measure of its complexity." So says the 1996 founding charter of The New England Complex Systems Institute (NECSI) in Cambridge, Massachusetts, written by Yaneer Bar-Yam.

One such complex system is the brain-mind connection and its RI.

Associated with NECSI is the International Conference on Complex Systems, which provides scientists, engineers, and social scientists with opportunities to rise above traditional disciplinary boundaries. In this environment they can explore the complexities of complex systems, sharing their respective mathematical tools to model and simulate a wide diversity of systems—physical, chemical, biological, social, and economic—with applications in areas such as psychology, civilization building, and management.

There are two key reasons for including this brief mention of NECSI, and its contribution to a branch of mathematical science called Complexity System Theory.

First, it is to emphasize that the sciences are enablers toward a fuller understanding of humans as the most complex living systems on Earth. Second, these diverse sciences include the fields of behavior, religion, philosophy, spirituality, and others that qualify as BTP.

Multitasking

The human brain-mind and RI have achieved such a high degree of complexity because they are very good—by design—at multitasking, or performing many functions simultaneously. And when interrupted, they can alternate between multiple tasks as well. To study this design feature, Dario D. Salvucci and Niels Aaatgen, both doctors of computer science, collaborated on an excellent reference based on their research, *The Multitasking Mind* (Oxford University Press, 2011).

Correlations, theories, and experiments

Because our brain-mind and RI make up a very complicated integrated system, researchers construct theories to explain its behavior. These theories are constantly reassessed and reconstructed in the light of new evidence from observations or experiments.

Studies are performed on the physical brain at the level of tiny microscopic neurons, or at the level of cellular tissue, and ultimately at its highest system levels.

Similar studies could be linked to the mind and RI, and here is where new research tools like correlations are most needed; these are statistical measurements to express the extent to which variables are related, and the nature of their relationships.

Laurence R. Tancredi, a psychiatrist-lawyer and Professor of Psychiatry at the New York School of Medicine, is uniquely qualified to address this burgeoning field. He is the author or coauthor of numerous articles and several books relating to law, ethics, and psychiatry. In *Hardwired Behavior: What Neuroscience Reveals about Morality* (Cambridge University Press, 2005) Dr. Tancredi advocates for more research on topics such as neuroscience and morality, morality and the mind, the biology of choice, and how to create a moral brain-mind connection.

"Over the past few decades extraordinary advances in neuroscience have accelerated the breakdown of the idea that a dichotomy exists between mind and body," he writes. "Taking these advances into account, as well as the likelihood of major breakthroughs over the next seventy-five to one-hundred years, this book concludes on a futuristic note—one involving eugenics—a concern that goes back to humanity's earliest moral percepts as articulated in ancient philosophy, in the Ten Commandments, and in the Seven Deadly Sins."

Modeling creativity, emotions, motivation, imagination, and behavior

At the hardware, or anatomical level, human brains are all quite similar. But at the software or mind level, every mind differs from every other mind.

This mystery is non-existent in all human-made systems, because they all share a one-to-one correspondence between the sophistication of their hardware and software.

Thus it's almost a waste of time to examine Einstein's brain (or that of Spock the Vulcan in "Spock's Brain," a famous episode of Star Trek) to see what made either the real or fictional character a genius. But it would be very useful if we were able to mathematically model the *living* human mind to study its creativity, emotions, motivations, and behaviors. Sophisticated mathematical models would allow us to include factors such as genetic makeup, up-bringing, environment, education, aging, and life experiences.

Advanced modeling could teach us, for example, how to better enhance creativity in children, or deal with a loss of motivation in old age.

Modeling emotions and behavior could reveal more about mental health issues, including depression and anxiety, and how BTP factors might be applied in prevention or remediation.

Trying to create all these characteristics within smart machines, however, is another waste of time, except in the anything-goes world of science fiction books and movies. The popular argument here is that if we improve the machine modeling and hardware/software to implement it, it will be possible to design machines capable of creativity, emotion, motivation, and other human-like behaviors.

As computer scientist Andrei Sorin notes in *Software and Mind: The Mechanistic Myth and its Consequences* (Andsor, 2013): "A calculator can add numbers correctly without understanding the meaning of addition as we humans do … there is no reason why a model that emulates simply mental acts, but working differently from a human mind, should reach even an average level of intelligence later when we improve that model."

In his excellent reference book, *Principles of Synthetic Intelligence* (Oxford University Press, 2009) Joscha Bach, an AI expert with a PhD in computer science, also deals with modeling creativity, emotions, motivation, and behavior. His 2006 PhD thesis was on *Principles of Synthetic Intelligence: Building Blocks of an Architecture of Motivation*.

Let us consider for example, whether human-like creativity can be integrated into that most familiar machine, the smartphone.

In *The Power of Intention: Learning to Co-create your World your Way* (Hay House, 2004) Dr. Wayne Dyer maintains: "People driven by intention are described as having a strong will that won't permit anything to interfere with achieving their inner desire."

Immediately in Dyer's words we can see how difficult it would be to define and measure intention and then duplicate it in an AI application.

Consciousness—computational neuroscience and mystic experience

All religious traditions highly recommend retreat experiences to restore the brain-mind connection to a healthy equilibrium. Judaism, for example, has Kabbalah, Islam has Sufism, and Christianity has many forms of monasticism.

This is not about escaping or avoiding life, but generating or rediscovering a new one, as is found in the Christian New Testament teachings of Jesus. Thus a spiritual retreat can never be negative; they are always subjectively positive. Some people even report mystic experiences. The retreat concept has become so desirable in our era that many non-religious people also seek it to achieve similar benefits.

While such benefits are hard to measure in the lab using modern brain imaging techniques, this should not stop scientists from researching them.

We understand consciousness as the physiological and cognitive state of being alert, awake, and fully aware of our surroundings. We also understand it as referring subjectively to one's identity, thoughts, morality, philosophy and meaning of life, and how we fit into this universe.

In her bestselling book *My Stroke of Insight: A Brain Scientist's Personal Journey* (Plum, 2006), Jill Bolte Taylor explains how she used to randomly select motivational Angel Cards "several times a day to help me stay focused on what I believe is important in life."

On December 10, 1996, Dr. Taylor, a 37-year-old neurologist with a post-doctoral fellowship at Harvard Medical School, experienced a massive stroke in the left hemisphere of her brain. Within just four hours, she could no longer walk, talk, write, or recall anything of her life.

But the stroke, which took eight years to recover from, was also a stunning revelation. It taught her that by "stepping to the right" she could uncover feelings of wellbeing and discover that inner peace is accessible.

Fifteen years later, she wrote *Whole Brain Living: the Anatomy of Choice and the Four Characters that Drive our Life* (Hay House, 2021).

Here, she further explains her use of Angel Cards: "The cards come in sets of assorted sizes with each card having a single word written on them (enthusiasm, compassion, joy, abundance, education, clarity, integrity, play, freedom, responsibility, harmony, grace, or birth …). Every morning when I first get up, I ritualistically invite an angel into my life and draw a card. I then focus my attention on that particular Angel throughout my day. I use the Angel Cards to shift me back into a state of being generous of spirit."

Denis Williams (1908–1990), a neurologist at St. George's Hospital in London, explains in his classic paper "Old and New Concepts of the Basis of Consciousness," that "consciousness is a state—a relative state—that cannot exist without a subject. In using a word which must be descriptive as though it were substantive, we go on to imply that consciousness has a neuronal system devoted to its maintenance, in the same way as the sense of sight has the retina, the visual pathway and cortex."

In Arabic, the word for consciousness has the same root as that for sight (as in insight). As we use our physical sight to appreciate beauty, enjoy the company of loved ones and protect ourselves from harm, we can use our consciousness (insight) to survive spiritually, to know ourselves and to love the entire universe.

In *The Kingdom of God is Within You: Christianity not Mystic Religion but as a New Theory of Life,* Leo Tolstoy (1828–1910) wrote: "We humans need to look at the savage brutalities of which our life is full, to be appalled at the contradictions in the midst of which we live, often without observing them. We need only recall the preparation for war, the mitrailleuses (machine guns), the silver-gilt bullets, the torpedoes, and the Red Cross, the solitary prison cells, the experiments of execution by electricity and the care of the hygienic welfare of prisoners; the philanthropy of the rich, and their life, which produces the poor they are benefiting."

Tolstoy, one of the world's greatest moral thinkers, was nominated for the Nobel Prize in Literature every year from 1892 through 1906, and for the Nobel Peace Prize in 1901, 1902, and 1909.

Despite all his nominations, he died without receiving a single Nobel honor, but his profound words remind us clearly that AI won't help us find peace of mind, the meaning of life, or peace and happiness when the human brain-mind has historically failed so badly in its collective efforts to do so.

In 1990 my friend Rabbi Dr. Reuven P. Bulka (1944–2021), Spiritual Leader of the Congregation Machzikei in Ottawa, gifted me an autographed and inscribed copy of his *Uncommon Sense for Common Problems: A Logotherapy Guide to Life's Hurdles and Challenges* (Lugus, 1989).

I also presented him with my *Spiritual Fitness for Life* (Pandora, 2004) which is now available free online (see link near the beginning of this chapter).

Dr. Bulka, author of more than two-dozen books, writes: "We have no proof that objective values exist. That there *are* objective values that follows from the foundations of existence. The human being, thriving in the health model, is directed toward meaning. If meaning were subjective, then it would not be unconditional; rather it would be dependent on subjective feeling. Therefore meaning must be objective." (Italics added.)

Moses Ibn Maimon (1138–1204), also known as Maimonides, served as Grand Rabbi of Andalusia but is buried in Cairo, Egypt, where he died. I am proud to own his *Guide for the Perplexed* in its original Arabic.

In the 1881 English translation by M. Friedlander, Maimonides writes: "Our knowledge is acquired and increased in proportion to the things known by us. This is not the case with God [whose] knowledge of things is not derived from the things themselves: if this were the case, there would be change and plurality … On the contrary, the things are in accordance with [God's] eternal knowledge, which has established their actual properties, and made part of them purely spiritual."

What beyond the physical isn't

BTP is not simply the flip side of the physical; similarly, spirituality is not the opposite of materialism, or even atheism. Both are programmed within the mind to create a sense of purpose and balance in life; this equilibrium relieves us of irrational or irrelevant dreams and obsessions, such as wanting to own a 50-room mansion.

In his *A Preface to 'Paradise Lost'* (Oxford University Press, 1942), the eminently sensible British lay theologian C. S. Lewis (1898–1963) wrote this about John Milton's (1608–1674) epic poem: "The first qualification for judging any piece of workmanship from a corkscrew to a Cathedral is to know *what* it is—what it was intended to do and how it is to be used. After that has been discovered, the temperance reformer may decide that the corkscrew was made for a bad purpose, and the communist may think the same about the Cathedral. But such questions come later. The first thing is to understand the object before you: as long as you think the corkscrew was meant for opening tins or the Cathedral for entertaining tourists you can say nothing to the purpose about them."

Clive Staples Lewis was also a writer, scholar, and academic who taught at both Oxford and Cambridge. Although he was talking about a specific piece of literary art in the foregoing excerpt, he offers an excellent methodology for knowing and judging anything, including one's own life. He guides us uncompromisingly to face questions such as: Who am I? Do I know myself? What was I intended to do in this universe? How do I make use of my potential? What is the purpose of life?

In *Religious Perplexities* (Hodder and Stoughton, 1922), L. P. Jacks (1860–1955) asks: "If we acknowledge that our existence has no purpose at all, would it not be futile to embark on inquiries concerning spirituality, God, freedom, duty, and Immortality? What meaning could these terms have for beings who had learnt that their own existence was purposeless? … The moment (a person) believes (their) divine origin, (they) acquire a new energy."

Dr. Jacks was an English philosopher, theologian, academic and Unitarian minister. He served as Principal of Manchester College at Oxford from 1915 until 1931 and wrote more than 50 books and articles.

Beyond the physical and sex

"Like a river that is regulated to avoid floods or drying up, love and even sex, carefully and usefully regulated, lose their wild, spontaneous, impractical beauty—though there is an undeniable utilitarian gain; which is what occurred in the relations between the sexes among Jews," wrote the late Dutch-American sociologist and Professor of Jurisprudence and Public Policy at Fordham University, Ernest Van Den Haag (1914–2002) in *The Jewish Mystique* (Stein and Day, 1969).

He adds: "Love is sweet, says a Yiddish proverb, but it's sweeter with bread … Jews never accepted the contempt of the body and its deliberate humiliation so characteristic of early Christianity. Jews could not afford contempt for a world to which they had to cling with all their strength, any more than a poor man can afford contempt for money."

Einstein and beyond the physical

It has become too difficult for any scientist to believe that our physical universe simply happened—it must have had a Creator, a *designing* one. Einstein was no exception.

The reasoning behind these two facts of faith—an originating creator, and a creation that was designed—is simple. Scientists experience first-hand that we discovered everything we know; *we didn't invent it.* They also know what it takes to design systems within systems, and that our universe is an amazing complexity of infinitely interwoven systems.

Scientists are actually very close to understanding the intricate, yet at the same time so simple and beautiful, design of our universe. The conclusion is that its original and continuing Designer must not only be infinitely intelligent, but the greatest creative artist of all time and existence.

Many scientists now use the language of faith, naming this unique designer as the Almighty, as God (in whatever languages have words for it). They understand that any design contains interrelated and sometimes even contradictory factors that must be skillfully and elegantly resolved in order for the overall design to function harmoniously. If there were multiple designers, optimum functionality and sustainability would be far more difficult, or even impossible.

Albert Einstein was just such a creative scientist. In 1905—a remarkable year for him and for science—he came so close to understanding the origins of matter that he could marvel at the Creator who set it all in eternal motion. From March through September that year, Einstein published five papers that transformed our understanding of nature or, as he put it, "God's thoughts."

John S. Rigden in his biography *Einstein, 1905; The Standard of Greatness,* writes: "Of all human activities, thinking is the single activity that most clearly sets us apart from other life forms. Thinking is what makes us humans ... Einstein's 1905 is an illustration of the thinking species at its best, the thinking person's standard of greatness."

Rigden goes on to explain the contents of Einstein's seminal papers: on the particle theory of light; on molecular dimensions; on the theory of Brownian motion; on the theory of relativity; and on the equation for which he is most famous, $E = mc^2$.

He quotes Einstein as saying, "What I'm really interested in is whether God [would] have made the world in a different way; that is, whether the necessity of logical simplicity leaves any freedom at all."

The great American physicist I.I. Rabi commented even more grandly that "Einstein was walking the path of God."

He describes how Einstein had to wait until experimental verifications confirmed his theories. On learning that one of them was accepted, he responded simply, "I knew the theory was correct." But when asked what if his theory had been refuted, he said; "In that case, I'd have felt sorry for God, because the theory is correct."

Einstein genuinely believed he had discovered what God allowed him to discover. For example, his iconic equation $E = mc^2$ seemed to come out of the blue. But he was pragmatically capturing the mass-energy relationship in radioactive material.

Rigden notes that Henri Becquerel discovered radioactivity in 1896, but the underlying physics of where the energy emitted by atoms came from remained a mystery until 1905.

Einstein thought that since radioactive energy might be produced at the expense of mass, the two could be related. The mass of a body is a measure of its energy content, so if the energy changes by E, the mass changes in the same sense, where E is divided by c^2.

Rigden quotes Jacob Bronowski from *The Ascent of Man* in which he writes: "It is almost impertinent to talk of (humanity) in the presence of two men; Newton and Einstein, who stride like gods. Of the two, Newton is the Old Testament god; it is Einstein who is the New Testament figure. He was full of humanity, pity, and a sense of enormous sympathy. His vision of nature herself was that of a human being in the presence of something god-like, and that is what he always said about nature. He was fond of talking about God."

Einstein indeed set the bar high for the interaction of faith and belief with the empirical demands of science; that is what makes his understanding of the divine Designer so compelling.

Logotherapy and the search for meaning

In 1959, *Man's Search for Meaning*, by psychologist and Nazi concentration camp survivor, Viktor E. Frankl (1905–2014), was published and since then has sold more than 16 million copies. In it, he discusses his approach to psychological therapy (logotherapy) by reporting on a conversation he had with an American colleague who asked him: Are you a psychoanalyst?

"I replied, not exactly a psychoanalyst, let's say a psychotherapist," he answered. "I follow my own theory; it's called logotherapy."

The American countered with another question. "Can you tell me in one sentence what is meant by logotherapy? … What is the difference between psychoanalysis and logotherapy?"

"Yes," Frankl said, "but can you tell me in one sentence what you think the essence of psychoanalysis is? (The American's) answer was, during psychoanalysis, the patient must lie down on a couch and tell you things which sometimes are very disagreeable to tell. Whereupon I immediately retorted with the following improvisation: Now, in logotherapy the patient may remain sitting erect but he must *hear* things which sometimes are very disagreeable to hear." (Italics added.)

Robin Williams, Sinead O'Connor and BTP

One of my favorite comedians was Robin Williams. I still remember hearing the news reports saying that Williams committed suicide on Monday, August 11, 2014 at age 61. Sadly, he was not unique, but just one of many high-profile stars in the entertainment world plagued by the demons of depression.

As I was finishing this chapter in July 2023, tragedy claimed another of my favorite artists, the Irish singer, songwriter, musician, activist, and passionate convert to Islam, Sinead O'Connor (1966–2023) at age 56. To cope with my grief and sadness I read her book *Rememberings* (Universal Mother, 2021) sending her a Rest-in-Peace-dear message as I did so.

Depression is a medical condition that affects the ability of a person to function in everyday life. Almost 10 percent of North American adults aged 18 and older experience some form of depression every year. Other Western nations are not far behind.

The symptoms include feelings of hopelessness, decreased energy, fatigue, anxiety, guilt, worthlessness, helplessness, loss of pleasure in activities once enjoyed, loss of interest in sex, difficulty concentrating, memory problems, indecision, insomnia or oversleeping, appetite and/or weight changes, suicidal thoughts, or suicide attempts.

Although therapy—which requires time, expertise, and money—can alleviate symptoms for more than 80 percent of those treated, less than half of those afflicted with depression can afford or access the help they need. Many patients and their doctors find it easier and faster to take medication as a sole means of alleviating the symptoms.

In fact, I was shocked to read an advertisement that a certain pill "ends depression and anxiety in less than 15 minutes." I am not a medical doctor but the claim sounds false to me, just like unverified claims for weight-loss pills that have been around for years.

There is no study to suggest that the percentage of Canadian Muslims who suffer from depression is higher or lower than that of the general public. But as a community elder and provider of pastoral counseling, I know the pain a patient goes through and how difficult it can be to obtain a timely referral to a health care professional.

There are indications that suggest Western societies have higher rates of mental illness than more traditional Arab, East Asian, African, and various Pacific Island societies.

Some studies indicate that an alarming number of men suffer from mental health problems, but most are culturally too "macho" to seek treatment, suggesting that more work is needed among men to destigmatize mental illness.

Although empirical data from many studies shows a strong correlation between physical/mental health and religious or spiritual practice, too much medical care today has degenerated into a one-dimensional and non-holistic model. Too often, mental health patients are told "take this medication and see me in a month," which allows doctors to cram as many consultations as possible into each day.

But four medical researchers led by Mark Townsend in the Department of Medicine at Virginia Commonwealth University rigorously reviewed medical research literature between 1966 and 1999 to examine the effects of religion on health. One of their criteria was that all four of the group had to read and approve each study before it could be included in their research, which was published in December, 2002.

One study concludes that Islamic-based psychotherapy speeds recovery from anxiety and depression in Muslims. Another indicates that religious beliefs and activities appear to benefit blood pressure, immune function, alleviate depression, and reduce premature mortality.

Yet another study found that Christian intercessory prayer appears to improve health outcomes in patients admitted to coronary care units and may improve survival in children with leukemia.

Among the findings of Mark Townsend's group are: private prayer may be associated with decreased depression after coronary artery bypass surgery among married men; religious activity may be associated with decreased depression among African Americans with cancer; religious involvement may be associated with fewer symptoms of depression among older Dutch men; religiosity may limit stressors in patients diagnosed with depression; and religious commitment may protect retired Catholic nuns from experiencing depression.

One very important conclusion was that "religion may also have a protective effect against suicide."

The Virginia researchers conclude that the vast majority of Americans consider religion as an important part of life and want health care providers to address faith and spirituality issues.

Townsend's group also concludes that "involvement in religion or religious activities may promote mental and physical health," including "promoting positive social and interpersonal functions, affirmation of shared beliefs, improving coping skills, resolution of guilt, diminished fear of punishment, (and) the threat of embarrassment."

They end their study with a very important recommendation. "Considering that patients think religion is important, that religion likely benefits health outcomes, and that religion is without financial cost, health care providers should include religion in the care of their patients."

Close-up fact

Appreciating beautiful things adds a lot to life, often in ways we may not even be aware of.

For further reading

Augustine of Hippo. *Confessions*. Hachette, 1961.

Ayala, Francisco J. *Am I a Monkey? Six Big Questions About Evolution*. Johns Hopkins, 2010.

Ball, Philip. Flow: *Nature's Patterns: A Tapestry in Three Parts*. Oxford University Press, 2009.

Bauman, Andrew. Wholeness: *How the Love of God Changes Us*. Navpress, 2018.

Benson, Herbert. *Timeless Healing: The Power and Biology of Belief*. Fireside, 1997.

Blackmore, Susan. *Consciousness: A Very Short Introduction*. Oxford University Press, 2005.

Bucaille, Maurice. *What is the Origin of Man?* Seghers, (1976) 1983.

Bucket, Richard Maurice, ed. *Cosmic Consciousness: A Study in the Evolution of the Human Mind*. Innes, 1905.

Burckhardt, Titus. *Alchemy: Science of the Cosmos, Science of the Soul*. Suhail, 1967.

Charlesworth, Brian and Charlesworth, Deborah. *Evolution: A Very Short Introduction*. Oxford University Press, 2003.

Cook, Joanna. *Making a Mindful Nation: Mental Health Governance in the Twenty-First Century*. Princeton, 2023.

Coulmas, Florian. *Identity: A Very Short Introduction*. Oxford University Press, 2019.

Crawford, Matthew. *The World Beyond Your Head: On Becoming an Individual in the Time of Distraction*. Penguin, 2015.

Descartes, René. *Discourse on Method and Meditations on First Philosophy*. David Weissman, ed. Yale, 1996.

Dingman, Marc. *Bizarre: The Most Peculiar Cases of Human Behavior and What They Tell Us About How the Brain Works*. Brealey, 2023.

Dyer, Wayne W. *The Power of Intention: Learning to Co-Create Your World Your Way*. Hay House, 2004.

Eagleman, David. *The Brain: The Story of You*. Vintage, 2015.

Eagleton, Terry. *The Meaning of Life: A Very Short Introduction*. Oxford University Press, 2007.

Einstein, Albert. *The World as I see It*. Snowball, 2014.

Elmasry, Mohamed. *Spiritual Fitness for Life: A Social Engineering Approach*. Pandora, 2004.

Field, Rashad. *The Alchemy of the Heart*. Element, 1990

Franck, Adolphus. *The Kabbalah: The Religious Philosophy of the Hebrews*. Citadel, 1979.

Frankl, Viktor E. *Man's Search for Meaning*. Beacon, 1959.

Frayn, Michael. *Plays: Copenhagen, Democracy, Afterlife*. Bloomsbury, 2010.

Freud, Sigmund. *Civilization and Discontent*. Norton, 1961.

Giuliani, Luigi. *The Religious Sense*. McGill, 1997.

Guénon, René. *The Reign of Quantity and the Signs of the Times*. Munshiram Manoharial, 1953.

Haeri, Shaykh Fadhlalla. *The Journey of the Self: A Sufi Guide to Personality*. Harper, 1989.

Haque, Amber and Yasien Mohamed eds. Psychology of Personality: Islamic Perspectives. International Association of Islamic Psychology, 2022.

Hall, Stephen S. *Wisdom: From Philosophy to Neuroscience*. Vintage, 2011.

Halpern, Sue. *Four Wings and a Prayer: Caught in the Mystery of the Monarch Butterfly*. Weidenfeld & Nicolson, 2001.

Heffernan, Margaret. *Willful Blindness: Why We Ignore the Obvious at Our Peril*. Bloomsbury, 2011.

Hick, John. *The New Frontier of Religion and Science: Religious Experience, Neuroscience and the Transcendent*. Palgrave, 2010.

Hick, John. *Disputed Questions in Theology and the Philosophy of Religion*. Yale, 1993.

Holland, John H. *Complexity: A Very Short Introduction*. Oxford University Press, 2014.

Hull, R.F.C. and A.S.B. Glover. *Aurora Consurgens: A Document Attributed to Thomas Aquinas on the Problem of Opposites in Alchemy*. Inner City, 2000.

Huxley, Aldous. *Brave New World*. Introduction by Margaret Atwood. Random, 2007.

Huxley, Aldous. *The Divine Within: Selected Writings on Enlightenment*. Harper, 1992.

Huxley, Julian. *The Struggle for Life: The Living Thoughts of Darwin*. Fawcett, 1959.

Huxley, Julian. *Religion without Revelation*. Mentor, 1927.

Izzo, John. *The Five Secrets You Must Discover Before You Die*. BK, 2008.

Jacks, L.P. *Religious Perplexities*. Hodder & Stoughton, 1922.

Kesavan, H.K. *Science and Spirituality: A Hindu Perspective*. AuthorHouse, 2003.

Kupperman, Joel J. *Philosophy: The Fundamental Problems*. St. Martin's, 1978.

Lanza, Robert and Bob Berman. *Beyond Biocentrism: Rethinking Time, Space, Consciousness, and the Illusion of Death*. BenBella, 2016.

LeDoux, Joseph. *The Emotional Brain: The Mysterious Underpinnings of Emotional Life*. Touchstone, 1998.

Le Fanu, James. *Why Us? How Science Rediscovered the Mystery of Ourselves*. Harper, 2010.

Lings, Martin. *Symbol and Archetype: A Study of the Meaning of Existence*. Fons Vitae, 2006.

Mahony, Kathleen. *Simple Wisdom: Shaker Sayings, Poems, and Songs*. Penguin, 1993.

May, Gerald G. *Care of Mind, Care of Sprit: A Psychiatrist Explores Spiritual Direction*. Harper, 1982.

McGrath, Alister. *The Big Question: Why We Can't Stop Talking About Science, Faith, and God*. St. Martin's, 2015.

Merton, Thomas. *The New Man*. Abbey of Gethsemane, 1961.

Mitchell, Roy. *The Exile of the Soul*. Blavatsky, 1981.

Moore, Thomas. *Meditations*. Harper, 1994.

Morowitz, Harold I. *The Emergence of Everything: How the World Became Complex*. Oxford University Press, 2002.

Moses, Maimonides. Guide for the Perplexed. Digireads.dot.com, 2018.

Niequist, Aaron. *The Eternal Current: How a Practice-Based Faith Can Save Us from Drowning*. Waterbrook, 2018.

Passingham, Richard. *What is Special About the Human Brain?* Oxford University Press, 2008.

Peers, E. Allison. *Dark Night of the Soul: A Classic in the Literature of Mysticism by St. John of the Cross*. Image, 1959.

Pink, Thomas. *Free Will: A Very Short Introduction*. Oxford University Press, 2004.

Proctor, Robert W. and E.J. Capaldi. *Why Science Matters: Understanding the Methods of Psychological Research*. Blackwell, 2006.

Richardson, Alan. *Religion in Contemporary Debate*. SCM, 1966.

Rigden, John S. *Einstein: 1905, the Standard of Greatness*. Harvard, 2005.

Rowlands, Mark. *The New Science of the Mind: From Extended Mind to Embodied Phenomenology*. MIT, 2013.

Rowlands, Mark. *Animals Like Us*. Verso, 2002.

Rowlands, Mark. *The Nature of Consciousness*. Cambridge University Press, 2001.

Rowlands, Mark. *The Body in Mind: Understanding Cognitive Processes*. Cambridge University Press, 1999.

Ruskin, John (1835). *On Art and Life*. Penguin, 2005.

Russell, Bertrand. *The Will to Doubt*. Welcome Rain, 1958.

Sabani, Meredith ed. *The Earth has a Soul: C.G. Jung on Nature, Technology and Modern Life*. North Atlantic, 2002.

Salvucci, Dario D. and Niels A. Taargen. *The Multitasking Mind*. Oxford University Press, 2011.

Schopenhauer, Arthur (1851). *The Wisdom of Life*. Dover, 2004.

Schopenhauer, Arthur (1850). *On the Suffering of the World*. Penguin, 2020.

Seneca (c. 49 CE). *On The Shortness of Life: Life is Long if You Know How to Use it*. Penguin, 2005.

Sense, Peter M. *The Fifth Discipline: The Art and Practice of Learning Organization*. Penguin, 2006.

Seth, Anil. *Being You: A New Science of Consciousness*. Faber, 2021.

Sheldrake, Philip. *Spirituality: A Very Short Introduction*. Oxford University Press, 2012.

Smith, Huston. *Beyond the Post Modern Mind*. Suhail, 2001.

Tancredi, Laurence. *Hardwired Behavior: What Neuroscience Reveals about Morality*. Cambridge University Press, 2005.

Taylor, Jill Bolte. *Whole Brain Living: The Anatomy of Choice and the Four Characters that Drive our Life*. Hay House. 2021.

Taylor, Jill Bolte. *My Stroke of Insight: A Brain Scientist's Personal Journey*. Plume, 2006.

Tolstoy, Leo (1894). *The Kingdom of God within You*. Kshetra, n.d.

Ud-Din Attar, Farid. *Conference of the Birds*. Arkana, 1974.

Wood, Bernard. *Human Evolution: A Very Short Introduction*. Oxford University Press, 2005.

Young, Shinzen. *The Science of Enlightenment: How Meditation Works*. Sounds True, 2016.

Healthy aging—
A travel guide

Right from the start, transparency is foremost here, for I have a major personal stake in writing this chapter.

First, I marked my 80th birthday on Christmas Eve, 2023 and in recent years, have lost dear family members and friends to cancer and Alzheimer's disease, all of them younger than me.

Second, as a long-time social activist, it has caused me great moral distress to have witnessed first-hand how persistently Canadian and American governments and their policy-makers have marginalized and even legislatively discriminated against the elderly. At no time in my life have I felt this more keenly than during the COVID-19 pandemic (2020–2023).

Third, as an Egyptian-Canadian who came to Canada as a PhD student in 1968—believing then that I was blessed to be living in the greatest country on earth—I was disappointed at how poorly this country treats its most vulnerable people; the indigenous, elderly, disabled, mentally ill, poor, racialized, women, and others. Sadly, too little has changed over the past half-century.

Fourth, as a leading academic and researcher in microchips and their applications to Artificial Intelligence (AI) and Artificial Neural Networks (ANNs), I know that the level of funding needed to truly advance scientific and medical research into the brain-mind connection, especially in geriatric studies, is nowhere near sufficient.

Funding cannot be met solely by not-for-profit organizations—government agencies must actively fill this gap, for the long-term good of all Canadians. Unfortunately, governments mainly fund research that will gain them more votes at election time and/or create a direct positive impact on the economy, like microchips and AI research.

DOI: 10.1201/9781003486848-7

But demeaning seniors as they grow older is not new.

In Act 2, scene 7 of *As You Like It*, William Shakespeare—who died at the ripe old age of 52, when the average male could expect to live only into his mid-30s—has the character Jaques recite what he called the "seven ages of man." The final stages paint a depressing picture of old age as "a bare, forked animal, lean and scant of breath," and ultimately, "sans teeth, sans eyes, sans taste, sans everything."

American novelist Ernest Hemingway (1899–1961) was just as uncomplimentary, calling *retirement* "the filthiest word in the English language."

Gladys Beryl Elder (1899–1976) wrote *The Alienated: Growing Old Today*, a classic about the bitter experience of her early 20th-century generation. No mainstream publisher would consider it, but fortunately the Writers and Readers Publishing Cooperative of London did. It came out in 1976, the year of her death.

Sadly, Elder (even her surname is a bleak irony) died alone in London's Victoria Hospital. I am proud to own a copy of *The Alienated*, stamped WITHDRAWN from the prestigious Library of Oxford University. In its 40 years of shelf life there, it had only *four* stamped borrowing dates.

English novelist John Boynton Priestley (1894–1984), co-founder of the Socialist Commonwealth Party, wrote prophetically in his Preface to Elder's *The Alienated*: "We have largely stopped seeing our old people simply as Grannie or Grandpa, but almost as members of a strange species, not at all ourselves simply further along in life. They are much more part of a problem or series of problems, rather than people who happen to have lived a bit longer than the rest of the population."

In the 1993 comedy movie *Grumpy Old Men*, lead character John Gustafson (played by Jack Lemmon) comments about a "lucky" friend, who had just died without going through the miseries of old age. "Son of a bitch!" Gustafson rants to equally grumpy pal, Max Goldman (Walter Matthau). "He went just like that (snapping his fingers). Give me a coronary any time!"

Anthea Tinker of City University, London, introduces *The Elderly in Modern Society* (Longmans, 1980) in these terms: "The elderly are particularly interesting to study. Not only are they one of the largest of what are labeled 'special groups,' but they are also the group to which in due time most people will belong."

David A. Bender, Emeritus Professor of Nutrition Biochemistry at University College, London, cites some disturbing 21st-century British figures in *Nutrition: A Very Short Introduction* (Oxford University Press, 2014).

In the early 20-teens, he noted, 3% of older United Kingdom men and 6% of older women who still lived on their own were undernourished. Shockingly, the statistics were even worse for those living in care homes, where nutrition would be an expected priority but was not. There, 16% of men and 15% of women were found to be significantly malnourished.

Today, these percentages are even higher in Britain, as well as in Canada and the United States. A pre-existing elder-care crisis was further exacerbated from 2020 on by drastic staff shortages at nursing homes in all three countries caused by the COVID-19 pandemic, along with a tidal wave of "quiet quitting" caused across the health services sector by chronically low wages and long working hours.

While we know that the physical and mental changes accompanying aging do not develop at the same time or pace for everyone, they must be studied in greater depth in order for care specialists to know more about what is normal and what is not.

There was a time when the elderly were revered as founts of knowledge and repositories of wisdom and were actively cared for by their families and communities, especially in indigenous societies. Now we live in an era obsessed with remaining young and with experiencing life through the latest and greatest in technological devices.

The public and media loudly proclaim outrage at the desperate plight of refugees, illegal immigrants, marginalized minorities, etc., and so they should. These are real humanitarian disasters. But equal attention should be devoted to *all* of us when we become old.

There has been growing public awareness of geriatric conditions such as Alzheimer's ever since US President George H. W. Bush declared the 1990s as "Decade of the Brain." But more than 30 years later, our discoveries in human brain-mind research have fallen far short of advances in smartphone and AI technology.

British surgeon Marjory Warren (1897–1960) is largely credited with founding the relatively new field of Geriatric Medicine, when in 1935 she took charge of the care of elderly patients at London's West Middlesex Hospital. The term geriatrics is derived from the Greek, meaning "old man healers."

Most medical schools now offer doctors special training in treating older patients with chronic and usually age-related medical disorders, such as high blood pressure, diabetes, arthritis, and various forms of dementia.

The bad news is that geriatrics, when mentioned in the popular media, focuses the younger public's attention on the high cost of elder care, causing frequent social and political pushback, with devastating moral implications.

In his excellent book, *Ageing* (Polity, 2013), Dr. Chris Phillips, Professor of Sociology and Social Gerontology at the University of Manchester, writes: "As we move further into the twenty-first century, it seems increasingly clear that momentum has slowed in the task of building a society that values and nurtures the possibilities and potential of ageing. Ageing continues to be viewed as a significant burden on western economies."

Unfortunately, I must agree with Dr. Phillips. I have lived among older people in four countries—Egypt, Malaysia, the United States, and Canada. I have found among North Americans in particular, a negative culture toward aging, even though they live in a much more affluent society. Again, the worldwide experience of COVID-19 (2020–2023) made that crystal clear.

Real-world fact

The COVID-19 pandemic years (2020–2023) exposed the entire planet to the serious inadequacy of cradle-to-grave healthcare. Care scarcity became shockingly evident in supposedly "first world" countries where seniors in nursing homes suffered far more than any other demographic.

It is time that Canadians and Americans demanded a radical overhaul of our respective governments' policies toward the elderly. Here is a partial list of actions drawn from my Canadian experience:

1. Just as family allowance supplements help low-income families bear the cost of raising healthy children, similar supplements should be provided for families so they can afford to take dignified care of their older relatives.
2. Just as we have the Children's Aid Foundation and/or Child and Family Services, we should have an equally effective and influential agency for older people. Canadian Association of Retired People (CARP) is a good start, but its advocacy campaigns on issues such as better long-term care standards, government-subsidized dental and optical care,

and higher old age security payments, need more support and response from government policy-makers, as well as from the younger public.

3. Most provinces offer various subsidies for working parents to defray the costs of child daycare, although there are still too few affordable spaces for low-income families. Similarly, a national day care program for seniors, especially those with dementia or conditions requiring constant supervision, would relieve care-giving families of some of the 24/7 burden. Current "respite" programs are too few, too infrequent, and too localized to be accessible to those who most need them. This is especially the case for "sandwich generation" adults who are trying to balance caring for their own children at the same time as their aging parents.

4. For generations children who were orphaned, or whose birth-parents were unable to care for them, have been raised in foster homes. While foster-homing for seniors with no living or nearby relatives has been successfully incorporated into the social programs of some European and Scandinavian countries, it has yet to be tried in Canada. A small but growing advocacy movement has emerged in recent decades but has yet to gain traction.

5. Early childhood education has been a successful component of our school systems for a long time, but not early "*second* childhood" education to any appreciable extent. Various experimental initiatives have shown that seniors with dementia can re-learn ways to cope with failing memories and other cognitive challenges, while also enjoying the benefits of socializing with their peer group and others in the community.

6. Seniors' discounts should be part of *every* business's standard practice, especially for essential services such as transportation, groceries, home repair/maintenance, and general retail. Government grant incentives could help smaller businesses with a narrow profit margin to offer such discounts.

7. While some limited tax credits are available to family members who care for their senior relatives, they are far too little to make much difference against the hard reality of today's steeply rising living, housing and service costs. And the credits that do exist are not well-publicized among those who could most benefit from them.

8. Western economies are buying into youth culture and age-denial big time, by moving their official retirement ages higher and higher; governments like the added "benefit" of avoiding paying longer-term pensions. Many seniors who are already "retired" are forced to continue working because corporate and government pensions have not kept

pace with the cost of living. Governments need to overhaul their old-age security programs and guarantee all retirees a living income.

9. Bingo halls, which offer only mentally and physically passive entertainment, could double as proactive social and learning centers where seniors could maintain in-person connections and acquire new skills.

10. Our schools should teach students about traditional family values, such as respecting older family members, learning from them, and helping to care for them, as is done to this day among Mennonites and other ethnic communities.

> **Real-world fact**
>
> In Western democracies, climate change has taken more space and time in election campaigns than improvements in seniors' care. We need to balance our attention to respond effectively to both issues.

The brain-mind connection in old age

Among a long list of diseases and conditions typically associated with aging—such as arthritis, hypertension, vision and hearing loss, cancer, diabetes, stroke, etc.—memory failure is universally considered the most devastating.

This is because losing your memories means losing your identity. You literally lose *you*. For your family, it is often like a slow death, a death so painful that they eventually avoid visiting or calling you.

Several years ago, after a long and successful career as an academic and researcher, a friend in his seventies was diagnosed with Alzheimer's. When I would meet him in social gatherings following his diagnosis, he was quiet; he had lost the ability to talk, to laugh, to smile as he always used to. He had traveled widely and once had thousands of interesting stories to share, but no more. All that rich experience was now locked inside a failing brain.

A year ago, his family decided to move him into a long-term nursing home. His wife, a retired nurse, could not take care of him anymore. I repeatedly asked my friend's son if he would take me to visit his dad. He kept promising but never did. I understand.

Developing at least some degree of memory loss is virtually guaranteed with advancing age. About 40% of those 65 or older will experience age-related memory impairment. In the United States alone, this amounts to some 16 million people annually, of whom about 1% will develop incapacitating levels of dementia.

About 1% of people 65 or older develop mild cognitive impairment (MCI) that can be managed successfully; but among that number nearly 15% will be diagnosed with Alzheimer's, whose degenerative process is inevitable.

As people live longer, their risk of developing Alzheimer's increases dramatically. As with all forms of dementia, the irreversible losses of dignity and identity are devastating. Although other conditions, such as lack of mobility, vascular disease, and respiratory ailments, also tax both patients and families, Alzheimer's remains at the top of the most-feared list.

My father died too young, of a heart attack in his fifties. I was only 16 and deeply saddened by his loss. I missed him a lot. He never got to see me become a leading professor and researcher in my field. He never saw any of his grandkids, including my four wonderful Canadian-born children.

My mother died 30 years later in her seventies, from dementia. She was able to enjoy being a proud and happy mother and grandmother. But her death was preceded by profound sadness. Eventually, she couldn't recognize me; she couldn't take care of herself; she didn't know if she was in Canada or Egypt. During the final year of her life, she recognized no one and no place. She was physically living, but mentally lost and it caused her family great pain.

The big question remains and will probably still hang over us, unanswered, long after you read this book: *Why is our elderly memory not as good as it was in our twenties, or even in middle age?*

And an even bigger question—*Why does advancing age mean inevitable physical and mental decline?*—is too difficult for most of us to even contemplate. But that has never stopped philosophers, theologians, and even biologists, from trying to find out just *why* we age and die.

Just over a decade ago, Pulitzer Prize-winning author Jonathan Weiner added his voice to a long tradition of immortality literature with *Long for This World: The Strange Science of Immortality* (HarperCollins, 2010).

Now if you believe, or even hope, that we humans might one day live forever (or even for a couple of centuries), or if you beg to differ, we can all benefit in the here and now by taking the best care we can of our aging minds, aging brains, and aging bodies.

But before we go into the how-to of strengthening our brain-mind-body connections, *we must accept a few hard facts* about aging.

The first is that our aging brain, the "hardware" containing our memories, has to work with fewer neurons than that of a twenty-something. Remember; unlike other cells, neurons don't regenerate or replace themselves, so damaged ones simply stop working. That means less memory capacity and longer retrieval time. It's a simple case of neurological and physiological "wear and tear."

The second is that our mind, the "software" containing our operating system, so to speak, along with the algorithms that manage our voluntary and involuntary memory functions, has been operating non-stop for some 50 or 60 years without any full-system "updates" like the ones our smartphones receive in the middle of the night. It's no wonder that the processor becomes sluggish after more than half a century of dealing 24/7 with other minds, stressors, relationships, challenges, or even traumas.

In her book, *Can't Remember What I Forgot* (Harmony, 2008) Sue Halpern writes that while memory loss is normal as we get older, "a diagnosis of mild cognitive impairment (MCI) [is] not, perforce, a sentence to die from Alzheimer's; some people went from MCI back to normal."

MCI is the stage between an expected age-related decline in memory and its impact on functions such as thinking, judgment, and language, and the more serious condition of declining into dementia.

Third, three factors impact our brains and minds at any age—genes, upbringing, and lifestyle. We have no control over the first two, but the third is dependent on choices we make during adulthood, preferably early adulthood.

As early in life as possible, we can make important lifestyle choices that will significantly *slow the rate of memory deterioration*. Instead of our memory hitting bottom in 50 years while we're still in relatively good physical shape, it could possibly serve us at a much higher level, even to the point where our physical bodies become too worn to function, perhaps past 100 years.

Did you know?

It is very beneficial to manage aging well and minimize many of the discomforts and restrictions that we often assume are "normal" with advancing years. But we must also realize that stopping the aging process altogether is impossible.

Is healthspan more important than lifespan?

Healthspan can be defined as the healthy period of one's life; that is, "being healthy from serious disease," that will cause death, says Tim Peterson, Professor of Medicine at Washington University, St. Louis.

In "Healthspan is more important than lifespan, so why don't more people know about it?" a paper published online (May 30, 2017) for the Harvey A. Friedman Center for Aging, Peterson lists ten serious diseases or conditions causing death among Americans, including Alzheimer's, various cancers and heart disease.

He calculated the average US healthspan to be 63 years, while the average lifespan was significantly longer, at 79 years. "This means that we, on average, live up to 20% of our lives unhealthy," he writes. "Needless to say, that is a long time."

To lengthen the first number in proportion to the second, Peterson emphasizes the critical importance of "maintaining a healthy balanced diet with moderate, regular exercise and without smoking and drinking alcohol." This, he argues, "is the surest way to promote one's healthspan and limit the onset of most diseases."

And in the years since his article, there has been a groundswell of renewed interest in and advocacy for the habit of daily napping, to replenish both mind and body.

Peterson adds that "social, intellectual, (spiritual) and physical activities are also huge healthspan determinants. Even though they may be more commonly associated with psychological effects, their strong physiological effects should not be ignored. They should be treated by medical professionals as frontline approaches alongside medicines."

Lifestyle tip

Planning for healthy aging must start early in life.

Now to some useful how-to tips for strengthening your memory.

What is good for memory is good for YOU

What is good for memory and the brain-mind is good for the body, and vice versa. It's good for all that is *you*.

This simple fact emphasizes that we humans are, as we say in engineering, comprised of systems-of-systems. And this is true at any age. Moreover, our existence goes far beyond the physical existence of any other sentient beings because of our self-awareness.

This means that a healthy brain, our hardware, needs a healthy mind, our software. This includes a healthy lifestyle; healthy behaviors, healthy planning, healthy thinking, healthy motivation, etc. Remember; health is *holistic*—physical, mental, and spiritual.

In 1984, when world heavyweight boxing celebrity Muhammad Ali (1942–2016) was diagnosed at age 40 with Parkinson's disease (he'd taken some 200,000 hits to the head during his career) he wrote *Healing* (Collins, 1996), a small yet beautiful spiritual book whose vision was to promote universal tolerance and understanding.

I was privileged to meet Ali in 1996 in San Francisco, where I was participating in the world's largest conference on microchips; it just happened to be at the same hotel where he was staying.

Ali was happy to meet a fellow Muslim with the same first name. He laughed and joked, calling me "brother Mohamed." We shared the same age group; he was born on January 17, 1942 and I was a little less than two years later, on December 24, 1943. He was an expert in the choreography of boxing—"float like a butterfly, sting like a bee"—and I was/am an expert on the miniature world of microchips.

Sadly, Ali died in 2016 at age 74. And here I am at 80, having just written a book on AI, Real Intelligence (RI), microchips, and the brain-mind connection. I hope Ali likes it: *To you my brother, the Greatest, with love.*

Review your lifestyle when young

It's difficult to convince someone in their 20s or 30s to review their lifestyle *now* so as to reduce the threat of Alzheimer's disease stealing their dignity, autonomy, and identity some 30, 40, or even 50 years later.

But here's an analogy to drive home the point.

Let's emphasize to young men and women how importantly lifestyle impacts their sexuality, in both performance and pleasure; this includes the viability and quantity of both sperm and eggs.

"When a man visits a sperm bank to make a donation," says Shanna Swan of Mount Sinai Medical Center in her book *Count Down* (Simon & Schuster, 2020), "certain lifestyle practices can quickly land him on the-no-fly list."

These practices can include using illicit drugs, taking certain daily medications, being infected with or exposed to sexually transmitted diseases, having same-sex partners, being exposed to certain occupational or environmental hazards, smoking, excessive alcohol use, nutrient deficiencies, being above or below the ideal weight range, and if they've developed sedentary "couch potato" forms of recreation.

"Yet most men are unaware of this," Dr. Swan continues. "Some lifestyle practices—such as smoking and heavy alcohol use—won't come as surprises because they're known to be harmful to your heart, lungs, bones, and other areas. But your doctor may not have mentioned—and your mother didn't know—that what's bad for these organs and tissues can be bad for reproductive function, too, kicking up the risk of problems with sperm quality in men, as well as with menstrual function, miscarriage, ovarian reserve, and other reproductive parameters in women."

Exercise your associative memory and nap to refresh it

The human brain-mind uses its memory very efficiently; it's preprogrammed from before birth to do that. Knowing how, why, and what information the brain-mind saves is important for healthy aging.

First, the brain-mind saves *only* what its programming says it needs.

Second, it uses *associative memory* (AM) techniques which require less storage space and retain the same amount of information.

Third, it *rewrites* anything it's been programmed to identify as being too important and valuable to lose.

Your brain-mind possesses these efficiency strategies naturally. It didn't have to borrow them from microchip designers—in fact, it's the other way around!

But what does it actually mean to "exercise" the associative memory? It requires you to upgrade your conscious awareness and turn your daily encounters with people and events into *full-life experiences* (FLE). This means engaging all five physical senses—sight, hearing, smell, touch, and taste—as well as your mental and emotional ones. This can be challenging to integrate into your life, especially as so many of us lapse into "autopilot" when involved in activities we consider mundane or simply boring.

But it's not only a worthwhile habit past mid-life; it can be a game-changer for adults of *any* age. This kind of heightened self- and environment-awareness is part of all good meditation techniques or meditation-based disciplines, such as yoga. It doesn't take long to acquire the *FLE* habit and there are many novel ways to do it.

Two proven methods of helping to rewrite (or, perhaps, rewire) your memory into FLE mode are through a good night's sleep and daytime napping.

In a recent research paper published in the scientific journal *Sleep* (Sleep Research Society, 2021), J. L. Ong and co-authors report: "After a habitual nocturnal sleep, participants who had a 90-minute afternoon nap encoded word pairs better than a comparable group who stayed awake. Nap time spindles may contribute to improve memory … We examined learning following a daytime nap compared with an equivalent waking period using fMRI and polysomnography."

A 2013 study by Rasch and Born, cited by Dennis et al. in the scientific journal *Learning & Memory* (2020) notes that: "Of the vast amount of information encoded each day, most of it will be forgotten. Only a few selected memories are retained for long-term storage. Sleep plays an important role in these memory consolidation processes."

And a 2019 paper by Van Schalkwijk et al. in the journal *Sleep Research* cites Diekel et al. from a 2009 report that: "Sleep appears to convey a benefit for associative memories."

As a personal experiment, try reading an "old-fashioned" hardcover printed book, rather than an e-reader version of it; let yourself underline significant passages and scribble comments in the margins (but use a pencil, especially if you borrowed the book!). Read impactful passages aloud, even if no one but the cat is listening; let laughter or tears happen when they will; breathe in the scent of the physical materials that the book is made of (paper, fabric, ink, glue, etc.); use your sense of touch to appreciate the texture and mass of the volume.

Remember the time, place, and circumstances of buying or receiving that book and perhaps even note them on the flyleaf or in a personal journal (another good habit). You see what just happened? You transformed the very ordinary event of reading into a *FLE*, one that enriched and exercised your associative memory.

With that experiment in mind, try applying the same heightened approach to other daily events.

Similarly, you can transform memories of loved ones, both family and friends, into *FLEs*. Remember where and when you've shared meals together, gone to movies, celebrated birthdays, had arguments (and made up afterwards), touched, kissed, or hugged.

Here is one area of learning where you don't need to wait for more research and scientific discoveries to prove that *napping refreshes, connects, and rewrites your memories; and turning people and events into FLEs enhances and exercises your memory.*

Take time to "Do Nothing" ... alone

We can all remember complaining, "Mom, I'm bored" and receiving a wise answer like, "Go and play by yourself," which didn't seem very helpful at the time. Often enough, our child-mind response was just another complaint, something like, "But there's *nothing to do!*"

As adults, however, we are often surprised to discover that taking time alone to reflect, in essence to "do nothing," comes with many long-lasting benefits. It's all about counting your blessings in life before you find yourself counting what you've missed.

In his classic book *Solitude* (Simon & Schuster, 1988), Anthony Storr writes: "Various schools of psychoanalysis assume that man is a social being who needs the companionship and affection of other human beings from cradle to grave. Yet the lives of creative individuals often seem to run counter to this assumption."

Storr cites Descartes, Newton, Locke, Pascal, Spinoza, Kant, Leibniz, Schopenhauer, Nietzsche, Kierkegaard, and Wittgenstein as some notable examples.

> ### Lifestyle tip
>
> Integrate a day for true rest into your week. Jews rest on Saturdays (Shabbat means "rest" in Hebrew), Christians rest on Sundays (sometimes called Sabbath, from the Hebrew), and Muslims rest on Fridays (called Ju'mah).

The power of passion

Try to do everything with passion. If you don't like washing dishes (who does?) but have to do it anyway, do it with passion. If you think that your boss doesn't deserve his position, you're probably not alone. But still, do your work with passion, for yourself and for the health of your memory. Remember how many unemployed people would be grateful for a boss, even one to complain about.

In *King of the Castle: Choice and Responsibility in the Modern World* (Islamic Texts Society, 1977) Charles Le Gai Eaton (1921–2010) wrote: "If, by some strange device, a man of our century could step backwards in time and mix with the people of a distant age, he would have good cause to doubt either their sanity or his own ... The sun's daily cycle, a raven's flight, mossy oaks, and water gushing from a glade would look familiar enough, but the meanings they carried for his new associates would be different."

Eaton was a British diplomat, writer, philosopher, and Sufi Master. He wrote several other books, including *Remembering God: Reflections on Islam* (Kazi, 2000) and *Islam and the Destiny of Man* (SUNY, 1985), among others.

In *The New Man* (Abbey of Gethsemane, 1961), Thomas Merton (1915–1968) confirmed that "doing nothing" nourishes the soul. "Just as some men have to struggle to recover a natural, spontaneous realization of their own capacity for life and movement and physical enjoyment, so all men have to struggle to regain the spontaneous and vital awareness of their spirituality, of the fact that they have a soul that is capable of coming to life and experiencing profound and hidden values which the flesh and its senses can never discover alone. And this spirituality in man is identified with the divine image in our soul."

Merton was an influential American Trappist monk, Catholic priest, writer, theologian, mystic, poet, activist, and scholar. In 2023, Columbia University opened the Thomas Merton Institute for Catholic Life at the Church of Notre Dame in New York City.

ARTS

Art, Reading, Travel, Sport—make up the handy acronym ARTS—for *all kinds* of art, reading, travel, and sport.

If you're not interested in the arts, it's time to get interested. I enjoy those large "coffee table" art books, not as décor accents, but to pore through and enjoy their imagery. Some of my reading choices even include comics; I may know all the humor by heart, but still laugh for the nth time. I have mentioned before how much I enjoy travel to different events and cultures and enjoy the memories from each trip. And I love to do my morning exercise while watching old live concerts of my favorite singers; they make my day.

Reading, both fiction and non-fiction, opens infinite new worlds that allow your brain-mind to travel far and wide in space, time, and feeling. You can complement reading with your own writing; you don't have to be a professional to create an original poem, story, or journal entry. Never under-estimate how much your memory is enjoying itself!

And travel doesn't have to be to the far reaches of the globe. For some amazing "armchair" trips, try video journeys with the popular and down-to-earth American public television guide and travel writer, Rick Steves, or the gritty make-do-and-carry-on escapades of Britain's Michael Palin, whose first career was as a member of the Monty Python comedy troupe. But if you are planning an in-person journey, take time to read about the history, culture, and people of your destination before you go. Above all, make sure to eat where the locals eat, at least once.

Interesting destinations can also be found much closer to home, easily within an hour's drive. Don't be like those Canadians living in our capital of Ottawa who have never visited the Parliament Buildings; or Americans living in their capital of Washington DC, who have never stepped inside the iconic Smithsonian Institute Museum.

In my home province of Ontario, there are Torontonians who've never ascended the CN Tower, marveled inside the Royal Ontario Museum, or viewed the masterpieces inside the Art Gallery of Ontario.

In my home country, there are Egyptians in Cairo who have never visited the Giza Pyramids close-up. And in my Canadian hometown of Waterloo, Ontario, there are long-time residents who have never explored the sur-rounding Mennonite community, attended a concert at Centre in the Square, or visited our local farmers' markets. Good travel starts where you are.

Sports are designed both to play and be watched. Now at 80 I only watch, but as a spectator I am still participating. I grew up in Cairo loving soccer, "the beautiful game," and still watch a match almost every day. I always make it a *FLE*. I watch with my sons and/or friends, either in-person or online in our respective homes. We laugh, joke, comment, argue, scream … Even when communicating only via text or audio messages, it's still good fun.

Walking and talking

Walking in cities is becoming increasingly difficult, even for fit and alert pedestrians. Imagine how it must be for elderly walkers. I know; I am one of them! Even light-controlled crossings require a quick step and good eyesight.

Added to increasing traffic congestion, is the accelerating disappearance of a primary reason why many elderly walkers used to enjoy their daily errands. Local small businesses and services, such as corner stores, delis, coffee shops, butchers, bakers (even candlestick makers), barbers, hairdressers, dentists, doctors, post offices, hardware stores, banks, and a host of others, have succumbed to factors such as staff retirements and high rents. Now you find most of them at the mall, miles (or in Canada, kilometers) away.

Despite these challenges, it's well worth it to learn about what is still available in your neighborhood and integrate those businesses and services into your daily walking routine. You not only benefit from the exercise but are supporting the local economy. Use all of your senses as you walk; make every step a *FLE*.

And, take time to share conversations with the people who serve you. Make it a regular habit and they will recognize you as a friend, going out of their way to serve you better because they know they are valued.

I learned this skill early in life and worked to become good at it. Now I can spontaneously ask my doctor about the interests of his university-aged children. I greet my German-speaking bank teller with my few words of German—*danke sehr*. I told my Iranian taxi driver how much I enjoyed visiting his beautiful country. I asked my massage therapist how was his trip to Ireland. I chat with my pharmacist about whether she will go on to graduate studies after her summer job. I praise my editor's pictures of her garden, which makes her forget about its persistent weed population. I tell my Indian-Canadian waiter that I enjoy cooking classic Indian dishes at home, such as korma.

I create sweet memories every day by encountering people as *FLEs*.

Lifestyle tip

Integrate giving into every part of your daily life. Money and "stuff" are only two of many gifts we can make and they are often not what other humans need the most. Even a smile, a friendly word, or a small caring gesture, can mean the world to your recipient, whether friend or stranger. And doing these small things creates happiness and fulfilment in you, too.

No pain, no gain

John Ruskin (1819–1900), one of the Victorian era's most celebrated writers, philosophers, and polymaths, famously wrote: "The law of nature is, that a certain quantity of work is necessary to produce a certain quantity of good, of any kind whatever. If you want knowledge, you must toil for it; if food you must toil for it; and if pleasure, you must toil for it. But (people) do not acknowledge this law; or strive to evade it, hoping to get their knowledge, and food, and pleasure for nothing, and in this effort they either fail of getting them, and remain ignorant and miserable, or they obtain them by making other(s) work for their benefit, and then they are tyrants and robbers." In today's language, Ruskin "nailed it."

In his bestseller *The Demon-Haunted World* (Ballantine, 1996) the great Carl Sagan (1934–1996), Professor of Astronomy and Space Science, Director of the Laboratory for Planetary Studies at Cornell University, and who hosted Cosmos—the first truly successful science-based TV series—recounted the gripping story of an obscure man called Frederick Bailey.

Bailey, an orphan, was brought up in slavery in Maryland in the 1820s. Sagan recounts how, later in life, Bailey described memories of his difficult past: "'It was a common custom to part children from their mothers ... before the child had reached its twelfth month.' He was one of countless millions of slave children whose realistic chances for a hopeful life were nil. What Bailey witnessed and experienced in his growing up marked him forever: 'I have often been awakened at the dawn of day by the most heart-rending shrieks of an own aunt of mine, whom [the overseer] used to tie up to a joist, and whip upon her naked back till she was literally covered with blood ... From the rising till the going down of the sun he was cursing, raving, cutting, and slashing among the slaves of the field ... He seem[ed] to take pleasure in manifesting his fiendish barbarity.' Bailey worked hard to teach himself how to read. Then he began teaching his fellow slaves. He used to say, 'Their minds had been starved ... They had been shut up in mental darkness. I taught them, because it was the delight of my soul'... He changed his name to Frederick Douglass (after a character in Walter Scott's *The Lady of the Lake*), eluded the bounty hunters who tracked down escaped slaves, and became one of the greatest orators, writers, and political leaders in American history."

Despite growing up in desperately deprived circumstances, the young boy and man who would become the famed Frederick Douglass understood Ruskin's philosophy of taking personal responsibility for overcoming the challenges that blocked the way to freedom for himself and countless other slaves.

From stress reduction to tranquility

"Several days of exposure to high levels of the stress hormone cortisol impair memory," reports the US National Library of Medicine's PubMed Central (https://www.ncbi.nlm.nih.gov/pmc/). "Chronic stress can contribute to depression and anxiety disorders, which often interfere with normal memory processing, particularly as people age."

"For things that are beyond my understanding, they are no concern of my understanding," asserted Stoic philosopher and onetime Roman emperor Marcus Aurelius (121–180 CE). "Once learn this, and you stand erect. A new life lies within your grasp. You have only to see things once more in the light of your first and earlier vision, and life begins anew."

If you become stressed easily and often over nothing, I recommend bestselling author Daniel Gladwell's *I Don't Give A F*ck* (Blossom, 2023). Yes, this is exactly the title—in bright yellow on a bright red background. He means it. Go ahead and get into it; you'll enjoy the ride.

Back to the wisdom of antiquity, Seneca (5 BCE to 65 CE) wrote in *On the Shortness of Life: Life is Long if You Know how to Use it*: "We are seeking how the mind can follow a smooth and steady course, well disposed to itself, happily regarding its own condition and with no interruption to this pleasure, but remaining in a state of peace with no ups and downs, that will be tranquility."

Perhaps Seneca and Aurelius, along with Gladwell, can remind us in our frantic 21st century that to overcome stress we must consciously choose when it's important to "give a f*ck" and when not to.

Physical activity

It's a well-established scientific fact that people who have been physically active between the ages of 20 and 60 show less risk for Alzheimer's disease later in life.

Be innovative in adding physical activity to your daily routines. During the COVID-19 lockdown, I switched my outdoor walk to counting steps indoors and doing stairs.

Because I spend much of my days sitting down while reading or writing, I got a dart board so I could stand up and challenge myself every two hours.

That inspired me to know more about how every muscle in my body functions and how I can take better care of them all. When I saw a copy of

The Student's Anatomy of Exercise Manual (Barron's, 2012) by Ken Ashwell, I bought it. It contains 50 essential exercises, all beautifully illustrated.

The Preface advises: "To help you memorize the location of various muscles and bones, the book contains an illustrated overview of the major body systems and a workbook featuring black-and-white line illustrations showing parts of the muscular and skeletal systems."

Dr. Ashwell is a professor of Neurobiology at the University of New South Wales (UNSW) Australia and is also the author of *The Brain Book: Development, Function, Disorder, and Health* (Firefly, 2012)

A healthy diet

The motto here is: What is healthy for the body is healthy for the brain.

People with excess body fat are at greater risk for diabetes and hypertension, leading to cerebrovascular diseases; these in turn often accelerate memory decline and dementia.

The Mediterranean Diet—emphasizing minimally processed plant-based foods, such as colorful fruits and vegetables, nuts, whole grains, legumes, and healthy fats (mainly olive oil)—is found to be very effective in preventing or greatly decreasing age-related cognitive decline. When necessary, vitamins and other supplements can enhance both physical and brain health.

Among some supplementary health-enhancing foods used by ethnic minorities in the US and Canada are arugula, a green added to salads; molasses for sweetening and iron; raw cocoa, added to coffee; bee pollen and "royal jelly"; spirulina; whole wheat bran, and plain yogurt. All of these and more are found in health food stores and ethnic specialty shops, and are increasingly easy to find in mainstream chain grocery stores.

The Healthy Brain (HarperCollins, 2017) and *Eat Well, Age Better* (Allen, 2012) by Dr. Aileen Burford-Mason, are highly recommended for understanding good food habits and their whole-body impact.

Smoking and alcohol

Your brain-mind and memory will thank you for avoiding smoking and alcohol. So much has been written about the dangers of both, that little needs to be added here. But whether you indulge or not, you may not realize that both habits significantly interfere with our ability to store, maintain, and retrieve information because they restrict blood flow, which supplies energy and oxygen to the brain.

Learn more, live better

Mental activities such as studying (any subject), learning languages, painting, listening to music, attending live theater or concerts, traveling, and reading all stimulate the associative memory.

In my 20s I taught myself squash, tennis, and swimming. I was not an outstanding athlete, but was good enough to join fellow graduate students in competitions. I also took lessons in painting, piano, and singing. I discovered that I had little talent for any of them, but the experience of learning enriched my memory, especially the inspiration of imagining that one day I could be a famous opera singer! Pavarotti and Michael Bublé beat me to it, and for that I'm grateful.

One thing I learned how to do well, however, was teaching Arabic to English-speaking students, both children and adults. Even though Arabic is my mother tongue, it was a challenge. After volunteering to teach at a local school, I wrote a curriculum and received Board of Education approval to offer my course as a high school credit.

Next, I proposed a similar course at my university (University of Waterloo) and it was also approved. To my surprise and delight, more than 50 students enrolled. It was the first time a non-linguistics professor with a specialty in microchips had taught any language there, let alone Arabic. The students gave me good reviews, and because there was continued demand for it, I handed the Arabic course over to the university's language faculty. Now, 30 years later, U of W has three levels of Arabic instruction.

Spirituality

For years, I was doubtful as to whether a science and engineering academic-researcher should venture very deep into the territory of religion and spirituality. But here I am.

We know that making good investments in our physical and mental fitness gives high returns at any age, but especially later in life. What about integrating spirituality into that investment?

A few years ago, as I reflected on the idea, the term "spiritual fitness" came to me. I liked it so much that I registered it as a trademark. Out of that came my book, *Spiritual Fitness for Life, A Social Engineering Approach* (Pandora, 2004) in which I try to answer the what, why, when, where, and how of spirituality, including how to measure it. In exploring this fascinating subject, I drew on Eastern and Western religious teachings, as well as from ancient philosophies and traditions.

Aldous Huxley (1894–1963) continually examined the spiritual basis of both the individual and human society, seeking in all his writings, whether fiction, non-fiction, or essays, to reach a balance between physical and spiritual life.

In the Introduction to Huxley's classic *The Divine Within* (1955), Professor Huston Smith quotes him as saying, "make the best of both worlds." Worded differently, Smith writes, "Huxley used to advise: Fair enough, one world at a time. But not half a world."

Smith also notes that "Huxley used to live with his wife at their cabin hide-away in the Mojave Desert. He used to take me for a long walk through its scrubby stretches … He loved the desert, he told me, for its symbolic power. Its emptiness emptied his mind. The boundlessness of its sands spreads a mantle of sameness—hence unity—over the world's multiplicity in the way snow does."

In 1960, Smith arranged for Huxley to give a series of lectures at the Massachusetts Institute of Technology, America's leading university of science and technology, and about as far away from traditional spirituality as you can get. The series proved so popular among students, faculty and the public that the Boston Police Department was called in to maintain order. Smith recalled that Huxley took the situation in stride, saying simply "It's because I've been around so long."

Rashad Field (1934–2016), the English Sufi master, used to say that spirituality has to be tasted to be appreciated. Field is credited with bringing the Sufis' famed Whirling Dervish music and dance and their Sema Ceremony, to Europe, Canada, and the United States. He authored more than a dozen books, including the bestseller *The Alchemy of the Heart* (Element, 1990), transcribed from thousands of hours of talks he gave around the world.

Don't bite off more than you can chew

This advice radically goes against the tide of our current culture. We're living in an age of high anxiety over the future; of economic and political uncertainty; of expectations from us at home, at school, and at work. We have no time for ourselves, no time to really get to know ourselves, to love ourselves, to enjoy ourselves, or even to fully take care of ourselves.

In *The Reign of Quality and the Signs of the Times*, René Guénon (1886–1951) wrote prophetically: "Among the features characteristic of the modern mentality [is] the tendency to bring everything down to an exclusively quantitative point of view." He wrote this (in French) in 1945. Nothing has changed in nearly 80 years!

Guénon is one of the great philosophers of the 20th century. Frithjof Schuon (1907–1998) said of him that "he had the central function of restoring the great principles of traditional metaphysics to Western awareness," adding that Guénon "gave proof of a universality that for centuries had no parallel in the Western world."

Schuon, a Swiss philosopher, poet, and painter wrote (also in French, like his earlier contemporary Guénon) more than 20 works on philosophy, spirituality, religion, art, and anthropology, including the classics, *The Transcendent Unity of Religions* (1948) and *Logic and Transcendence* (1970).

He was an avid disciple of Guénon and went on to influence a number of great scholars of the following generation, including Martin Lings, Titus Burckhardt, Hossein Nasir, William Stoddart, and Huston Smith.

Time is on your side; just do a reset

The good news is that you can start a lifestyle of healthy aging at *any* age—it is never really too late. You can approach it proactively, in much the same way as good drivers operate their vehicles defensively. Aging and its twin, gravity, can both be on your side.

The great German philosopher Arthur Schopenhauer (1788–1860) wrote: "In the realm of actuality, however fair, happy and pleasurable we may find it, we are nonetheless always under the influence of gravity, which we have continually to overcome in the realm of thought; on the contrary, we are disembodied minds, weightless and without needs or cares. That is why there is no happiness on earth to compare with [that] which a beautiful and fruitful mind finds in a propitious hour in itself."

In other words Schopenhauer, back in the 18th century, realized that there is always time for a reset, so that the mind can transcend all that weighs it down.

Older and wiser? Absolutely!

Award-winning author Stephen S. Hall devoted his entire book *Wisdom: From Philosophy to Neuroscience* (Vintage, 2011) to address the topic of wisdom and aging. Researchers have shown there is a difference between older and younger adults in their cognitive approach to problem-solving, especially problems that are socially and emotionally charged. These are precisely the situations that often demand (however loosely we define it) "wise" decisions.

Recent psychological research shows that older adults are more comfortable dealing with uncertainty and ambiguity than younger ones—one of the fundamental traits of wisdom.

Older adults are also suppler in processing problems, as they can more readily perceive the social context of a situation and adjust their responses to it. And more importantly, they show greater flexibility in settling on an action strategy due to having developed better control of their emotions.

This kind of comparative behavioral research shows that neuroscientists may have indeed discovered solid empirical evidence for age being a bona fide source of wisdom. "With age comes wisdom" is no longer simply a proverb.

Close-up fact

Traditional and Indigenous cultures have always valued the wisdom of their elders and cared for them with the respect and love they deserve. The value of elder wisdom should be renewed in every society and be taught in schools. Children and elders form some of the most productive and joyful partnerships of all.

Less AI, more RI

When I asked my grandkids, currently aged 10–15, "What is one-third of nine?" they had to use the calculator app on their smartphones to find the answer. After they'd spent a week with their parents on the beaches of Cuba, I asked them to name the capital city of the island country they'd just visited. They had to use the search engine on their smartphones.

Like most of their generation, they are far from "stupid" (after all, they are *my* grandkids!), but they are not using their RI. Instead, they've come to rely on the AI apps in their smartphones. They have detoured around exercising their brain-mind connection, including their memories. By contrast, their parents are keen that they exercise their bodies; each one participates in at least three sports after school.

Now imagine soccer players training by using passive simulators, instead of running, jumping, and kicking the ball out on the field. It would be unthinkable in any organized sport. The players' actual physical performance levels would be embarrassingly bad.

Why do we expect anything different when we overuse AI apps on our smartphones instead of training and exercising our brain-mind connections? A healthy memory goes hand-in-hand (or neuron-in-neuron) with RI. Our memory simply can't reach its full potential without RI.

Remember to live, not live to remember

Keeping our memory working well, especially when we cannot become completely immune to age-related memory disorders, is only one part of a happy and fulfilling life. Life itself is a mystery continually being discovered.

Remember; *your age is measured by how much you discover every day, not biologically by how many earth rotations you've accumulated.*

At age 90, the renowned English playwright Michael Frayn, FRSL (b. 1933), republished three of his classic plays, *Copenhagen* (1998), *Democracy* (2003), and *Afterlife* (2008). He also wrote a new Introduction and Postscript to them. This is unusual for a playwright.

"If justification is still in the end needed for piling acknowledged fiction on top of the already ambiguous structure of fact," Frayn wrote, "it's surely this: that all those internal states and events that so affect our perceptions and recollections—all our fears and hopes, our preconceptions and self-deceptions—cannot themselves be directly observed … Our intentions are often even more elusive. And yet, without some understanding of the intentions behind it, no human action can be judged, or even made sense of."

In his beautiful book, *Meditations; on the Monk who Dwells in Daily Life* (HarperCollins, 1994) Thomas Moore (b. 1940) writes: "Meditation offers innumerable ways to leave the here and now for the forever. This kind of meditating may last only seconds—as you glimpse a woodpecker climbing up a tree outside your window."

Moore has been a monk, a musician, a university professor and a psychotherapist, as well as the author of more than 30 books, including the bestselling *Care of the Soul: A Guide for Cultivating Depth and Sacredness in Everyday Life* (HarperPerennial, 1992). He has a PhD in religion from Syracuse University and has been awarded several honorary doctorates.

He says of *Meditations* that it "… attempts to capture that Alchemy for the reader. I believe we all, men and women, have much to gain by reflecting on religious community life as a spirit that can be fostered within our ordinary, secular lives. It is a spirit that can deepen our values and experiences, nourish our souls, and reveal sacredness where one previously suspected only secularity."

Close-up fact

When our mothers, fathers, or other trusted elders advise us to "do your best and let God to do the rest," we should trust in their wisdom as an essential key to living without anxiety.

Add your own wisdom

Now it's your turn. What advice and tips would you add to our list? Send them to us at www.iMindNow.co and we will publish a representative selection.

For further reading

Ali, Muhammad and Thomas Hauser. *Healing: A Journal of Tolerance and Understanding*. Collins, 1996.

Bender, David. *Nutrition: A Very Short Introduction*. Oxford University Press, 2014.

Bennett, Jane. *The Enchantment of Modern Life: Attachments, Crossings, and Ethics*. Princeton, 2001.

Bulka, Reuven. *Uncommon Sense for Common Problems: A Logotherapy Guide to Life's Hurdles and Challenges*. Jason Aronson, 1990.

Carrol, Noel. *Humour: A Very Short Introduction*. Oxford University Press, 2014.

Cohen, Elwood. *Alzheimer's Disease: Prevention, Intervention, and Treatment*. Keats, 1999.

Cook, Joanna. *Making a Mindful Nation: Mental Health and Governance in the Twenty-First Century*. Princeton, 2023.

Elder, Gladys. *The Alienated: Growing Older Today*. Writers and Readers Cooperative, 1977.

Gladwell, Daniel. *I Don't Give a F*ck: Improve Your Life by Ditching the Bullsh*t*. Blossom, 2023.

Goldbloom, David. *We can do Better: Urgent Innovations to Improve Mental Health Access and Care*. Simon & Schuster, 2021.

Halpern, Sue. *Can't Remember What I Forgot: The Good News from the Front Lines of Memory Research*. Harmony, 2008.

Hersey, Tricia. *Rest is Resistance: A Manifesto*. Little Brown, 2022.

James, Nicholas. *Cancer: A Very Short Introduction*. Oxford University Press, 2011.

Philippines, Chris. *Ageing*. Polity, 2013.

Restak, Richard. *The Complete Guide to Memory: The Science of Strengthening Your Mind*. Skyhorse, 2022.

Sagan, Carl. *The Demon-Haunted World: Science as a Candle in the Dark*. Random, 1997.

Storr, Anthony. *Music and the Mind*. Ballantine, 1992.

Summerhill, J.K. *Take Charge of Your Life*. Hawthorn, 1968.

Swan, Shanna H., with Stacey Colino. *Count Down: How Our Modern World is Threatening Sperm Counts, Altering Male and Female Reproductive Development, and Imperiling the Future of the Human Race*. Scribner, 2020.

Thompson, John M. *Arthritis*. Key Porter, 2005.

Tinker, Anthea. *The Elderly in Modern Society*. Longmans, 1981.

Wills, David. *Prosthesis*. University of Minnesota, 2021.

The future—A balancing act

Earth, this beautiful planet of ours, has been spinning on its axis and orbiting the sun for more than 4.5 billion years and could very well be around for at least another few billion. Each complete rotation literally takes a day out of the life of everything on it and in it—including us.

While humans have lived on this planet for some 300,000 years, that enormous timespan represents a mere 0.007% of Earth's entire existence.

That's right; for nearly all of its history our home world has spun along without us. It took *that long* for it to develop the kind of habitat in which we could survive and multiply—the right temperature, gravity, and air pressure; as well as enough fresh water, breathable atmosphere, edible plants, animals to hunt and domesticate, raw material resources, and so on.

Humans have been preprogrammed from birth to look after one another, to be caring stewards of Earth and even the entire Universe. What an honor and responsibility!

We don't know how long Earth will keep spinning around the sun. All we can know for sure is that one day it *will* stop; and on that day life on this beautiful globe, if there still is any, will cease to exist.

In the present tense, we know that the amazing human brain-mind-Real Intelligence (RI) collaboration is here to stay, after evolving for hundreds of thousands of years. And today we are fortunate to possess the knowledge that can keep this unique "machine" in lifelong optimal health for as long as we live—but *if and only if* we take care of our own brains and those of others.

The computing and communicating "smart" machines we have collectively designed and produced are also here to stay. And we have the choice of using or abusing them.

DOI: 10.1201/9781003486848-8

The world of smartphones, microchips, and AI Apps is still young but they, like us, will continue to mature. They were born in our research labs and factories as the result of accumulated and accessible knowledge that has been saved and dispersed ever since the advent of the Gutenberg printing press in 1440. Before that, it was difficult, often impossible, for anyone but the very wealthy to gain access to past knowledge.

Many ancient civilizations reached remarkably advanced levels in arts, sciences, and oral/aural literature, but few attained sufficient written literacy to produce books for future generations to read.

Short of nuclear war or planet-wide environmental catastrophe, humans will continue to benefit from the accumulated knowledge of at least the past 5,000 years, as well as adding to it.

One of my dreams is that universities will introduce both undergraduate and graduate interdisciplinary courses that will integrate in-depth studies of the brain, mind, and RI with an equally intensive study of the technologies of smartphones, microchips, and Artificial Intelligence (AI).

Carver Mead (b.1934) et al. of Caltech were credited with launching a revolution in microchip systems in the classic textbook, *Introduction to VLSI* (Addison-Wesley, 1979).

Following the success of this book, they focused on mimicking the human brain-mind as an analog system by introducing the then-novel concept of Neuromorphic Engineering. It took some time for this discipline to gain academic traction, but Steve Farber reported recent advances in the field in 2016 in *The Journal of Neural Engineering*.

Clark Elliott, author of the bestselling *The Ghost in My Brain: How a Concussion Stole my Life and How the New Science of Brain Plasticity Helped me Get it Back* (Viking, 2015), observes: "It is important to know that we are only starting to learn about how the brain works—from a computational standpoint it is roughly equivalent to 50 million computers and we know very little about its actual design. I would like readers to gain some appreciation for the true magnificence of the human brain and its profound capabilities."

Elliott has been a professor of AI and Cognitive Science at DePaul University for more than three decades. As a performing artist (and onetime child prodigy) he also studied at the Eastman School of Music. He has authored many research papers on computational models of emotion and personality, on believable software agents, and on cognitive neuroscience. He is also one of the first academics to have developed process models for Intelligent Agents.

In *The Ghost in My Brain* Elliott recounts his harrowing experience of surviving and healing from a serious concussion resulting from a car crash in 1999. During the long journey to recovery, he kept a journal that grew to 1,200 pages of detailed documentation. He continued this journey by speaking to more than 10 million people about his experience and the new neuroscience of brain plasticity.

Elliott has gone on to develop and teach more than three-dozen new courses in computer science, cognitive science, and ethics. In his work, he often refers to two important books by Norman Doidge, *The Brain's Way of Healing* (Penguin, 2016) and *The Brain that Changes Itself* (Penguin, 2007).

In *Insects in Flight* (McGraw-Hill, 1968), Werner Nachtigall, Professor and director of the Zoological Institute at the University of Saarlandes, writes: "As recently as the end of the nineteenth century, flying-machines were built in the shape of gigantic birds. But Nature does not present us with blueprints from which engineers can borrow indiscriminately."

He continues: "Engineers should learn a great deal by studying how nature has solved many technical problems, but they cannot take nature's solutions and use them without adaptation. They must observe and compare, pick up ideas but not copy them slavishly, work upon them, and use them as starting points. The branch of research called 'bionics'—or biotechnology—has precisely this for its object; researchers can eavesdrop on the secrets of nature."

Richard Passingham in *Cognitive Neuroscience: A Very Short Introduction* (Oxford University Press, 2016) reflects: "It is tempting to speculate about technical advances that might be possible that could revolutionize cognitive neuroscience."

Dr. Passingham is an Emeritus Professor of Cognitive Neuroscience at the University of Oxford and was among the first to use brain imaging to study human cognition. His other books include *What is Special about the Human Brain?* (Oxford, 2008), and (with James B. Rowe) *A Short Guide to Brain Imaging* (Oxford, 2015).

He emphasizes that brain activity needs to be studied "with methods that are sensitive to the temporal pattern of neuronal activity. But neither PET nor fMRI (are) well suited for the purpose because the blood supply does not change as rapidly as the activity of the neurons themselves. This means that we will need to exploit other methods and there are currently three that are available: Magneto-encephalography (MEG), Recording with electrode arrays, and Recording from single neurons."

He asks: "What of the future for the longer term? No one believes that all we need to do to understand the brain is to use brain imaging or record from neurons. There are an estimated 100 billion neurons in the human brain. Thus we need models of how the brain works that we can run on supercomputers … (L)et us suppose that is done. Will that be psychology or will it be neuroscience? The question is much like asking whether molecular biology is physics, chemistry, or biology. Like molecular biology, cognitive neuroscience lies at the borders between different disciplines, and that is where the excitement so often lies in science. Much more exciting than studying the behavior of rates and pigeons."

Susan Hockfield, professor of neuroscience at MIT—the first woman *and* first life scientist to head the prestigious institute—turned a lecture on "The Twenty-First Century's Technology Story: The Convergence of Biology with Engineering and Physical Sciences," into *The Age of Living Machines: How Biology will Build the Next Technology Revolution* (Norton, 2019).

"The path I've traveled, side by side with so many other scientists and engineers, has been enormously enlightening and rewarding," she writes, "but there's still far to go. The future looms. We still face daunting challenges in the coming century, and to overcome them we will need to summon up a shared ambition and shared commitment that are every bit as powerful as the one that we summoned up to win the Second World War. But this time, I fervently hope, we will be motivated not by the threat of war, but the promise of peace."

The future of machines: market or technology driven?

Manufacturing a machine can be market driven; that is, in direct response to consumer needs. In other cases, it is technology driven, used to manufacture specialized machines that consumers have little or no need for, due to their high cost (or complexity). But in other cases, markets are created alongside the advances offered by new machines and their technologies. In reality, most machines end up being both market and technology driven.

But one example of a technology driven machine designed for, but rejected by consumers, was a 1980s home phone with a video screen allowing people to see one another as they conversed. Cartoon shows like *The Jetsons* featured videophones, but the iconic movie, *2001: A Space Odyssey* gave this futuristic technology an everyday warmth when a space-traveling scientist videophones home to talk to his young daughter on earth (https://www.youtube.com/watch?v=ZjCDMc22IAM). Audiences everywhere loved that scene in the 1960s, even though the concept was far ahead of its time.

But in the 1990s, another technology driven communication machine, the mobile wireless device (soon to be called the cellular phone), seemed to come along at just the right time to be immediately accepted by consumers. As the phones rapidly decreased in size and price, and increased in reliability and features, worldwide usage expanded exponentially and continues to do so.

Will the numerous available AI Apps for today's smartphones continue to grow the global population of users? It's safe to predict that growth will continue for the next decade or so, but slow down somewhat as we reach the mid-21st century.

A currently popular smartphone trend is wireless hardware attachments that measure blood pressure, blood sugar, weight, movement, energy expenditure, etc. All this personal health data is stored and easily down-loaded to be plotted graphically on a daily, weekly, or monthly basis.

Similarly, the growing Internet of Things (IoT) will expand as more and more stationary furnishings and appliances become programmed with Apps that allow them to function when users are far from home. Today's "smart homes" feature remotely controllable conveniences such as heating/AC thermostat panels, lighting systems, cooktops and ovens, refrigerators and freezers, security cameras, etc., all of which can communicate with your smartphone, and vice-versa. On an even larger scale, hospitals, schools, universities, and businesses of all sizes from corner stores to multinational corporations are increasingly connected through the IoT.

In the not-too-distant future the IoT could link not only individual smart homes, but also smart neighborhoods, smart communities, and smart cities.

One challenging technical problem that must be resolved urgently is to efficiently manage the huge amount of data traveling over wireless net-works. Solutions are still in the research stage using the same computer sciences of machine learning (ML) and Big Data (BD) that are currently used in developing new AI Apps.

Prostheses and imaging technologies

Thanks to medical progress through AI and smart technologies, the near future will witness major advances in prostheses—replacement parts for full or part organs, joints, and complete limbs. Knee and hip joint replacements have become almost commonplace and heart pacemakers are also routine. Cataract operations, in which clouded natural eye lenses are replaced with plastic ones, have also become textbook medical procedures. Diagnostic advances enabled by enhanced imaging technologies have played a vital role in moving each of these life-changing operations from research to everyday reality.

In his visually beautiful 1995 book *Prosthesis*, David Wills, professor of French and Francophone Studies at Brown University, explores the human body as a technological marvel, seamlessly integrated, physically and psychologically, with modern prosthetics.

His ideas are further developed in two other books; *Inanimation: Theories of Organic Life* (2016), which explores the many meanings of being "alive" and *Dorsality: Thinking Back through Technology and Politics* (2008), which investigates how technology functions "behind or before" the human. All three titles are published by the University of Minnesota.

The future of RI

The diverse balance between human spirituality and our materially driven existence determines individual answers to such fundamental questions as: Who are we? What do we want? Where do we go? What do we do? Or see? Or remember?

And in our future existence on planet Earth, creating a beneficial balance between using our RI and the AI in our smart machines will play a vital role in how long and healthy that future will be.

At the collective RI level we should reflect on the 1956 words of C. Wright Mills, Professor of Sociology at Columbia: "Only when mind has an autonomous basis, independent of power, but powerfully related to it, can mind exert its force in the shaping of human affairs. This is democratically possible only when there exists a knowledgeable public, to which people of knowledge address themselves, and for which (people) of power are truly responsible."

Nurturing our RI

An amazing function of human RI has been the ability to create oral communication in order to survive. Even more amazing is that we learned further how to create symbolic structures to write and preserve most of our oral languages, and then to teach others, accumulate more knowledge, discover, govern, record history, etc.

Language has launched wars and created peace treaties. It has also given humans a limitless imaginative tool for writing poems, great litera-ture, songs, and plays. Although we are born not knowing how to speak or communicate through words, those abilities are preprogrammed into our RI in the womb. Language skills such as talking are acquired mainly through unsupervised learning; babies imitate what they hear.

Reading and writing our aurally acquired languages, however, requires supervised learning. In many ancient civilizations, literacy skills were con-sidered sacred and could be accessed only by the wealthy and elite. But social and cultural barriers never stopped poets, playwrights and others from recording their stories and verses to share with all, including those who could not read or write.

The history of language—spoken, read, and written—is an endlessly fas-cinating subject. Steven Roger Fischer wrote three excellent books in the field, all of which have gone through several editions (only the earliest are given here): *A History of Reading* (2003), *A History of Writing* (2001), and *A History of Language* (1996).

Fischer (b. 1947) is a New Zealand linguist and former Director of the Institute of Polynesian Languages and Literature at Auckland. He also authored *Island at the End of the World* (Reaktion, 2005) about the turbulent history of Easter Island, a place I just put on my bucket list.

Fischer's work has been praised by the preeminent linguist Noam Chomsky (b. 1928), who writes that his "intriguing and ambitious study explores a vast terrain, parts of which have scarcely been charted, oth-ers examined in some depth over many years and, as he relates, many centuries. Throughout, he addresses hard questions that bear directly on fundamental and distinctive aspects of human nature and achievement. A stimulating and highly informative inquiry."

Beware—Human RI can be weaponized

Humans can use their RI to influence and control the RI of other humans. This technique is often referred to as "brain-washing," and can cause per-manent psychological damage. By contrast, a machine programmed with AI cannot change or influence the cognitive processes of another AI machine—

at least, there has been no evidence so far of such machine-to-machine influence.

In *Battle for The Mind: A Physiology of Conversion and Brain Washing* (Doubleday 1957; Malor 2015) William W. Sargant asks: "How could it be that people would suddenly change their long-standing common sense?"

"In brain-washing," he explains, "trauma is applied through sleep deprivation, relentless pressure of an alternative ideology, and physical abuse. In religious conversion the trauma is internal, a conflict between fear of hellfire and damnation, versus acceptance of the new religion. In spirit possession, there is no trauma, but the pressure of heightened emotional pitch that comes from repetitive drum-beating, chanting, dancing, and drug or alcoholic use."

Sargant (1907–1988) was a leading British-American physician and researcher in psychological medicine.

Stop and smell the roses

Whenever I felt down or "blue," my late mother was right on target when she would advise me, "stop and smell the roses my son!"

In *Landscapes of the Mind: Worlds of Sense and Metaphor* (U of T Press, 1990) J. Douglas Porteous expands on that time-tested maxim spoken by numerous mothers down through history.

In his beautiful book, with original drawings by Ole Heggen, he discusses the joys of Smellscape and Soundscape, then delves into Bodyscape, Mindscape, Inscape, Homescape, Travelscape, Escape, Childscape, and Deathscape, drawing from abundant references such as philosophy, literature, poetry, geography, psychology, and even urban and environmental studies.

Dr. Porteous is Professor of Geography at the University of Victoria, in British Columbia, Canada.

The brain-mind in medicine

In 2009, Stanley Joel Reise wrote an important book *Technological Medicine: The Changing World of Doctors and Patients* (Cambridge University Press). Reise is a clinical professor of Health Care Sciences and Health Policy at George Washington University School of Medicine and Health Sciences. He is a prolific author, with more than 120 books and essays to his credit.

In *Technological Medicine*, Reise advocates for what he calls "a different kind of CPR (concepts, policies, and relationships)" to effectively govern the new empire of machines in medicine. He argues that there are "three basic steps to harmonize the technological with the social and humanistic spheres of medicine."

1. "We should evaluate the adequacy of the current theoretical basis of medicine. There are advantages of an adaptive concept which views health and disease as outcomes of the interactions individuals are having with environments encircling their lives—mainly the outer physical and social worlds and the inner personal and mental one. Accommodative responses to the challenges of these environments are synonymous with wellness, just as unaccommodative ones are with illness. The adaptive perspective was a basic component of Hippocratic medicine and lasted for a very long time. An adaptive perspective resists the inclination to view a person's health condition narrowly. Anatomical interests can be incorporated into this approach but cannot dominate it."

2. "To master the technology we must establish strong medical relationships. They generate evidence and resolve problems that technological interventions cannot. Only when the theory explaining health and illness requires relationships and dialogue to thrive will learning the essence of who we are and what we need as patients become a prominent and constant feature of medical encounters."

3. "A third step necessary to encourage the measured use of technology is cogent social policies. Examples are giving fixed payments to treat particular medical problems, regardless of how many technological and other interventions are made, in an effort to limit unnecessary therapies; and assessing the effectiveness of technologies in terms of their cost, benefits, and burdens compared to alternative treatments, in an attempt to determine the best therapy for given conditions. While essential, as the main agents used to guide technology, social policies have been ineffective. This is because without alternative ways to conceptualize illness that provide non-technological paths to understand and treat patients, physicians will resist placing limits on what they view as their first and most dependable option—technological measures. How can they do otherwise?"

Our brain-mind and climate change

More than two decades ago William H. Calvin (b.1939) wrote *A Brain for all Seasons: Human Evolution and Abrupt Climate Change* (University of Chicago, 2002) concerning the impact of climate change on our brain-mind.

Dr. Calvin is affiliate Professor of Psychiatry and Behavioral Sciences at the University of Washington School of Medicine in Seattle. He has written or coauthored more than 20 books, including (with George A. Ojemann) the important reference text, *Inside the Brain* (New American Library, 1980).

Calvin warns that: "When 'climate change' is referred to in the press, it normally means greenhouse warming, which, it is predicted, will cause flooding, severe windstorms, and killer heat waves. But warming could also lead, paradoxically, *to abrupt and drastic cooling* ('Global warming's evil twin')—a catastrophe that could threaten the end of civilization." (Italics added.)

He adds: "About 120,000 years ago, in the warm period that preceded our most recent ice age, modern type Homo Sapiens was probably walking around Africa with dark skin—and sporting a brain that was three times larger than before (the) ice ages … Now it's not obvious what ice has to do with brain size requirements."

More conferences are needed

To transition safely into this new age of AI without compromising human RI, interdisciplinary conferences among researchers are essential. Some have already occurred, but they have been too few in number compared to the pace at which technology is expanding.

One such event held in Foggia, Italy (January 19–21, 2022) was titled, "First International Conference, PLT '22; Psychology, Learning, Technology."

Among the topics addressed were: The Motivation of Distance Learning in Universities; Storytelling Practice in Sectors of Education; Psychology, Communication and Marketing; E-learning Platforms; Robot Assistive Therapy Strategies for Children with Autism; and Empowering Students to Shape Their Future.

The proceedings of PLT '22 were edited by Drs Pierpaolo, Raffaele Di Fuccio, and Giusi Antonia Toto (Springer 2022).

Our future, our choice

It has been 50 years since world renowned economist E. F. Schumacher (1911–1977) wrote *Small Is Beautiful: A Study of Economics as if People Mattered* (Abacus, 1973). Schumacher prophetically argued that a price has to be paid for anything worthwhile, to redirect technology so that it serves us instead of destroying us. And that requires a balancing act, an effort of the imagination, and the abandonment of fear.

Finally...

Here we come to the end of the journey that you as a reader, and I as an author, have traveled together. If you believe in the "cosmos of communication" as I do, I feel I already know you as a fellow human interested in the dreams and science that prompted me to write this book.

I thank you for a beautiful journey and hope we meet again in the future.

If there is any sound advice I can give to my younger readers after having spun 80 years, and hopefully more, on this beautiful planet Earth, it is what my mother said. She lived long enough to see her son reach the top of the world of microchips and AI research; she knew that I was in demand as a consultant all over the globe—Japan, Europe, the United States, and all across Canada. And she reminded me: *"My son, it's easy to make a living, difficult to make a difference."*

Truer words were never spoken. So it is my sincere hope that many young people from all walks of life, all cultures, all circumstances, all faiths, and all disciplines, will find and read this book. I hope someone will give them a copy for graduation or for their birthdays. I want them to be fluent in understanding the smartphones they use, the microchips that made those smartphones possible, the sciences behind all of that and behind the AI Apps they have access to.

Knowledge has always been, and always will be, the key to turn challenges into opportunities. We all share the lifelong responsibility of leaving this beautiful spinning planet Earth at least as lovely as we found it, and hopefully better. I hope this book becomes a catalyst for young people to achieve even greater knowledge, the kind that makes a difference, so I have gathered a list of recommended references for further reading. I wish the coming generations a happy future.

I also hope that I have given my older readers enough knowledge to help them overcome their many fears about the future, to reduce depression and anxiety, and embrace a positive lifestyle of healthy aging.

Finally, I hope that *all* my readers, wherever they are on the continuum of life, will find a hobby, a passion, or a sport they love—in which the skills to excel will come from the harmonious interaction of brain-mind and body.

I hope they will be inspired in this way to take care of their physical, mental, and spiritual wellbeing and achieve a truly whole-life experience. I hope they nourish love within, tasting the sweetness of every breath and enjoying the myriad beauties of this universe.

I would like to close by quoting Thomas Merton:

> We do not exist for ourselves alone, and it is only when we are fully convinced of this fact that we begin to love ourselves properly and thus also love others. What do I mean by loving ourselves properly? I mean, first of all, desiring to live, accepting life as a very great gift and great good, not because of what it gives us, but because of what it enables us to give to others.

Happy spinning everyone!

For further reading

Ashwell, Ken. *The Brain Book: Development, Function, Disorder, Health*. Foreword by Richard Restak. Firefly, 2012. This is a beautifully produced book about the human brain. Dr. Ashwell is Professor of Neurobiology at University of New South Wales, Australia.

Attia, Peter. *Outlive: The Science and Art of Longevity*. Harmony, 2023. Dr. Attia's book is a recent #1 New York Times bestseller.

Benson, Herbert. *Timeless Healing: The Power and Biology of Belief*. Fireside, 1997. Benson, a cardiologist, was professor of Mind/Body Medicine at Harvard and founder of The Mind/Body Institute at the Massachusetts General Hospital. This book, now considered a classic, offers an evidence-based approach to physical and mental healing through spirituality and prayer.

Bloom, Paul. *Psych: The Story of the Human Mind*. Harper, 2023. Dr. Bloom is Professor of Psychology at the University of Toronto and at Yale. This well-written book is a recent and accessible addition to the field.

Burford-Mason, Aileen. *The Healthy Brain: Optimize Brain Power at Any Age*. Harper, 2017. Dr. Burford-Mason is a cell biologist and former assistant professor in the Faculty of Medicine, University of Toronto. The book emphases nutrition as a natural way to achieve optimal mental health and wellness.

Butler, Gillian et al. *Managing Your Mind*. 3rd ed. Oxford University Press, 2018. This is the latest printing of a popular 700+ page reference whose first edition was published more than 20 years ago. *Managing Your Mind* is "for building resilience, overcoming emotional difficulties, and enabling self-development."

Buzsaki, Gyorgy. *The Brain from Inside Out*. Oxford University Press, 2019. Dr. Buzsaki is Professor of Neuroscience at the New York University School of Medicine. This book is a follow-up to his classic *Rhythms of the Brain*, where his thesis is that the human brain probes its physical surroundings to select only the information it needs to survive and flourish.

Calvin, William H. *A Brain for All Seasons: Human Evolution and Abrupt Climate Change*. University of Chicago, 2002.

Dingman, Marc. *Bizarre: The Most Peculiar Cases of Human Behavior and What They Tell Us about How the Brain Works*. Murray, 2023. Dr. Dingman is Professor of Biobehavioral Health at Pennsylvania State University; this book includes case studies on some of his patients.

Dreyfus, Hubert L. *What Computers STILL Can't Do: A Critique of Artificial Reason (AI)*. MIT, 1992. Dr. Dreyfus was Professor of Philosophy at the University of California, Berkeley. This MIT edition is a re-release based on the original 1979 edition. Dreyfus also authored *Mind over Machine: The Power of Human Intuition and Expertise in the Era of the Computer* (Free Press, 1988). In his books Dreyfus argues why the very idea that a machine can display human-like understanding is mistaken.

Eliasmith, Chris. *How to Build a Brain: A Neural Architecture for Biological Cognition*. Oxford University Press, 2013. Dr. Eliasmith holds a Canadian Research Chair at the University of Waterloo in Theoretical Neuroscience and is director of the UW Centre for Theoretical Neuroscience. He also holds appointments and cross-appointments in the UW Departments of Philosophy, Systems Design Engineering and Computer Science, and Psychology. His book mathematically analyzes brain functions, especially memory, attention and planning.

Elmasry, Mohamed I. ed. *VLSI Artificial Neural Networks (ANNs) Engineering*. Kluwer, 1994. Dr. Elmasry is Emeritus Professor of Computer Engineering at the University of Waterloo and was the founding director of its Microchips Research Group. This book explains the mathematics behind the design of ANNs (forerunners of AI) to mimic brain functions.

Fischer, Steven R. *A History of Writing*. Reaktion, 2021.

Fischer, Steven R. *A History of Reading*. Reaktion, 2019.

Fischer, Steven R. *A History of Language*. Reaktion, 2016.

Greene, Brian. *Until the End of Time: Mind, Matter and Our Search for Meaning in an Evolving Universe*. Knopf, 2020. Dr. Greene is Professor of Physics and Mathematics at Columbia University. He is the author of many scientific reference books.

Greenfield, Susan. *A Day in the Life of the Brain: the Neuroscience of Consciousness from Dawn till Dusk*. Allen, 2016. This book explains how the brain manages our lives over a 24-hour day.

Greenfield, Susan. *Mind Change: How Digital Technologies are Leaving their Mark on our Brains*. Penguin, 2014.Dr. Greenfield is a neuroscientist and member of the UK House of Lords. *Mind Change* stirred national controversy when she claimed that the human brain "is under threat from the modern (digital) world."

Greenfield, Susan. *You and Me: The Neuroscience of Identity*. North Hill, 2011. This book discusses identity from varied social, psychiatric and neuroscience perspectives.

Greenfield, Susan. Foreword. *Inside the Body: Fantastic Images from beneath the Skin*. Firefly, 2007. The book offers in unprecedented detail, color images from inside the body's organs, including the brain, using advanced imaging technologies, each with a brief informative description.

Hawkins, Jeff. *A Thousand Brains: A New Theory of Intelligence*. Basic, 2022. Hawkins is a pioneer in the field of handheld computing devices. In this book he proposes new architectures for intelligent machines.

Hockfield, Susan. *The Age of Living Machines: How Biology will Build the Next Technology Revolution*. Norton, 2019. Dr. Hockfield is president emerita and Professor of Neuroscience at the renowned Massachusetts Institute of Technology; she was the first woman ever to head MIT. In this book, she highlights advances in computer-engineered crops, virus-built batteries and cancer-detecting nanoparticles.

Kissinger, Henry A., Eric Schmidt and Daniel Huttenlocher. *The Age of AI and Our Human Future*. Little Brown, 2021. Schmidt was Google CEO and Chair (2001–2011); Huttenlocher is inaugural dean of MIT's Schwarzman College of Computing; Henry Kissinger was US Secretary of State and national security advisor under presidents Richard Nixon and Gerald Ford. This book ponders "what AI will mean for us all."

Matronic, Ana. *Robot Universe: Legendary Automatons and Androids from the Ancient World to the Distant Future*. Sterling, 2015.

McGilchrist, Ian. *The Matter with Things: Our Brains, Our Delusions, and the Unmaking of the World*. Perspective, 2021.

McGilchrist, Ian. *The Master and His Emissary: The Divided Brain and the Making of the Western World*. Vols. 1 & 2. Yale, 2010. In these three books totaling some 3,000 words, Dr. McGilchrist, a prominent psychiatrist, philosopher, and literary writer, examines the relation between neuroscience and metaphysics.

McKibben, Bill. *The Flag, the Cross, and the Station Wagon: A Graying American Looks Back at His Suburban Boyhood and Wonders What the Hell Happened*. Holt, 2022. Oxford University Press. *Very Short Introductions*. This series includes more than 300 concise volumes on wide-ranging scientific topics and is considered an excellent and informative source of "stimulating ways into new subjects."

Poynter, F.N.L. ed. *The Brain and its Functions*. Blackwell, 1958. This classic book contains 18 research papers on the brain/mind, presented at the Anglo-American Symposium, July 15–17, 1957.

Plotting, Henry. *Evolution of Mind: An Introduction to Evolutionary Psychology*. Penguin, 1997.

Ratey, John J. *A User's Guide to the Brain: Perception, Attention and the Four Theaters*. Vintage, 2002. Dr. Ratey is associate clinical Professor of Psychiatry at Harvard Medical School. Although a best-seller when published over two decades ago, it does not relate the brain and the mind to recent advances in AI and microchip technology.

Reiser, S.J. *Technological Medicine: The Changing World of Doctors and Patients*. Cambridge University Press, 2009.

Restak, Richard. *The Complete Guide to Memory: The Science of Strengthening Your Mind*. Skyhorse, 2022. This is the latest of more than 20 books Dr. Restak has authored about the human brain.

Sargant, William. *Battle for the Mind*, Malor Books, 2011.

Seth, Anil. *Being You: A New Science of Consciousness*. Faber, 2022. Dr. Seth is Professor of Cognitive and Computational Neuroscience at the University of Sussex, UK. His research focuses on the biological basis of consciousness.

Glossary

Algorithm A finite set of rules applied to calculations or problem-solving, particularly for programming and preprogramming smartphones or computers. The term can be borrowed in modeling the human brain-mind.

Analog In data systems, smartphones, or computers, analog refers to the use of signals to present information, expressed in any value between an upper and a lower limit. This method of presenting information is used by the human brain-mind. In the case of machines, analog signals are converted into digital signals (signals that take only two values, zero and 1) for easy processing and storing of information; for this the Analog to Digital Converter microchip is used. To make digital information intelligible to the human brain-mind, digital signals are converted into analog signals using Digital to Analog microchip devices.

App Short for Application; a computer program designed for a specific purpose, especially when used in smartphones. The term can be borrowed in modeling the human brain-mind.

Artificial or Machine Intelligence (AI) A computer program that performs actions that mimic the decision-making capabilities of the human brain-mind by learning from large sets of examples.

Artificial Neural Networks (ANNs) ANNs are electronic networks whose design and operational principles mimic the biological neural networks in the human brain-mind. This level of machine learning evolved into AI.

Associated memory A method of organizing, saving, and storing information in smartphones, computers, or in the human brain that uses related (i.e., associated) information in order to conserve memory space.

Backpropagation algorithm An algorithm used to train artificial neural networks whose design and function are borrowed from the human brain-mind. The ANN can correct itself to improve predetermined learning results.

Bug An error in a computer program or algorithm; also called a "glitch," or "gremlin."

Belief A strongly held religious, philosophical, and/or lifestyle proposition.

Central Nervous System In humans, a dense central aggregation of nerve tissue, consisting of the brain and spinal cord.

Cerebral cortex In humans, it is the outer layer of the brain's two hemispheres and largely responsible for our behavior.

Cerebral hemispheres The left and right portions of the human brain.

Cerebrum The largest part of the human brain, comprising the bilateral cerebral hemispheres.

ChatBot A computer program installed on smartphones, tablets, or laptop computers to carry on a conversation using predetermined questions and answers. Chat is from chatting. Bot from robot.

Cognitive science The interdisciplinary scientific study of human mental processes through fields such as linguistics, psychology, neuroscience, philosophy, artificial intelligence, and anthropology, among others.

Deep learning This is part of the family of machine learning methodologies based on Artificial Neural Networks and can have many levels of programming.

Digital In data systems, smartphones, or computers, digital refers to the use of discrete (binary) signals, zero or 1, to present information. This method of presenting information isn't used by the human brain-mind.

Gene A unit of hereditary information carried in cell chromosomes, transferred from parent to offspring, which determines some characteristics of succeeding generations.

Hardware The tangible or physical components that make up a smartphone, or a computer, in contrast to the intangible component of software, or programming.

Image recognition In both humans and smart devices, the function of recognizing, and responding to, visual images.

Machine Learning (ML) The development and application of algorithms that can solve problems without further programming instructions, by adapting and "learning" through repeated examples, with or without direct human intervention.

Microchip An integrated collection of miniaturized electronic circuits, comprised of transistors and other components, arranged on a small wafer or "chip" of silicon.

Mind This is the part of the human brain which is responsible for self-awareness. It thinks, imagines, remembers, senses, and determines what is to be learned and recorded.

Memory The part of the human brain or AI device (such as smartphone or computer) where information is recorded and stored.

Model A system, thing, or phenomenon used as a template or example to emulate. Models are used in the analysis of human brain-mind functions.

Neuron Neurons are the nerve cells that form the building blocks and connective system of the human brain. They are responsible for receiving sensory input from the external world and from internal memory; sending electrical motor impulses to muscles; and for executing thought processes.

Perceptron This is a single artificial neuron, programmed to switch on when its input exceeds a predetermined value. Perceptrons are important components of machine learning.

Plasticity In brain science and biology, plasticity is the inherent ability of a living organism to adapt to or be shaped by its environment, especially when that environment undergoes changes that could threaten its survival. Scientists are discovering how important neuroplasticity is in helping the brain heal from a wide range of traumas.

Preprograming This is the process of installing programmed instructions and functions on a smartphone, computer, or other electronic device to control its future actions; it usually takes place at the manufacturing stage to make these devices more user-friendly and accessible. The term can be borrowed in modeling the brain-mind.

Program A program is a sequence of instructions coded so that a computer or smartphone can understand and perform them repeatedly over an indefinite time period. Software may include many interrelated programs. Computer programs that can be read by humans are called Source Code. This term can be borrowed in modeling the brain-mind.

Real Intelligence (RI) This is the cognitive capability preprogrammed into the human brain-mind before birth; it allows us to develop and learn throughout our entire lives.

Refreshing memory   In smartphones, computers, and the human brain-mind, it is the process of reading information from stored memories and "rewriting" it.

Robot   A robot is an electro-mechanical device, often (especially in Science Fiction) resembling a human or domestic animal. It is controlled by internal and/or external computer programs allowing it to repeatedly carry out physical and computational actions.

Short-term memory   Information retained in the human memory for brief periods of time which, if repeatedly reviewed, becomes embedded in long-term memory as learning. The term is also used in software engineering.

Singularity   A state in which known laws no longer apply, creating distortions. Black holes in space are commonly called singularities. A singularity can happen in any complex system, physical, biological, etc.

Smart sensor   Smart sensors use embedded microchips to perform the preliminary processing of information that they collect from the external environment before sending it to a central location. This term can be used in studying the sensing capabilities of the human brain-mind.

Software   Software is a generic term for the collection, or suite, of programs making up the intangible component of smartphones or computers. It consists of sets of instructions, data, or purpose-built algorithms that execute specific tasks.

Supervised learning   Supervised learning is an approach to AI in which the algorithms of smartphones or computers are trained to find answers or perform new functions through their internal programming. The term can be used in studying the human brain-mind which, for example, is supervised when we learn to read.

Training   In machine learning, a device's programming is trained to create its own results by being provided with numerous examples of what is required.

Training dataset   This is often an extremely large amount of data used in machine learning to train AI programs how to solve problems on their own. From the training dataset, machine learning algorithms extract features that are relevant to their specific functions.

Unsupervised machine learning   This is a machine learning approach in which human programmers do not directly "coach" algorithms to find answers, but instead let them learn through analyzing and comparing numerous datasets in order to extract useful patterns. It is an important feature of AI technology. The term can be used in studying the human brain-mind; humans, for example, learn to talk through unsupervised learning.

Theory   This is a substantiated explanation of observed data that can incorporate laws, hypotheses, and measurable facts.

Transistor   This is a miniaturized semiconductor, usually mounted on a silicon chip, which can operate as both an on-off switch and an amplifier; it is used to regulate the flow of electronic signals and is the main building-block of microchips.

Vacuum tube   A vacuum tube consists of a filament in a sealed glass bulb. When the filament is heated, it causes electrons to become active. Before transistors were invented, vacuum tubes were used to control the flow of current in electronic devices and also as on/off switches in the first computers.

References

Chapter 1: Introduction

Anderson, John R. *How Can the Human Mind Occur in the Physical Universe?* Oxford University Press, 2007.

Bar-Yam, Yaneer and Ali A. Mini, eds. *Unifying Themes in Complex Systems, Volume II: Proceeding of the Second International Conference on Complex Systems.* Perseus, 2004.

Belofsky, Nathan. *Strange Medicine: A Shocking History of Real Medical Practices Through the Ages.* Penguin, 2013.

Bloom, Paul. *Psych: The Story of the Human Mind.* HarperCollins, 2023.

Burke, James. *Circles: 50 Round Trips Through History, Technology, Science, Culture.* Simon & Schuster, 2000.

Bury, J.B. *A History of Freedom of Thought.* Williams, 1800.

Bynum, William. *The History of Medicine: A Very Short Introduction.* Oxford University Press, 2008.

Calvin, William H. *A Brain for All Seasons: Human Evolution and Abrupt Climate Change.* University of Chicago, 2002.

Calvin, William H. *How Brains Think: Evolving Intelligence, Then and Now.* Basic, 1996.

Cobb, Matthew. *The Idea of the Brain: A History.* Profile, 2021.

Davies, Paul. *The Mind of God: The Scientific Basis for a Rational World.* Simon & Schuster, 1992.

Eddington, Arthur Stanley. *The Nature of the Physical World.* MacMillan, 1929.

Epictetus, c. 90 CE. *The Art of Living: The Classical Manual on Virtue, Happiness, and Effectiveness.* Harper Collins, 1944.

Fromm, Erich. *Psychoanalysis and Religion.* Yale, 1950.

Greene, Brian. *Until the End of Time: Mind, Matter, and Our Search for Meaning in an Evolving Universe.* Knopf, 2020.

Kant, Immanuel. *Groundwork of the Metaphysic of Morals.* Harper, 1948.

Laslett, Peter, comp. *The Physical Basis of Mind: A Series of Broadcast Talks.* Blackwell, 1950.

Le Fanu, James. *Why Us: How Science Rediscovered the Mystery of Ourselves.* Harper, 2010.

Matthews, Dale A. and Connie Clark. *The Faith Factor: Proof of the Healing Power of Prayer.* Penguin, 1998.

Moscovitch, Morris, ed. *Infant Memory: Its Relation to Normal and Pathological Memory in Humans and other Animals.* Plenum, 1984.

Nadler, Spencer. *The Language of Cells: A Doctor and His Patients.* Vintage, 2002.

Nicolelis, Miguel. *Beyond Boundaries: The New Neuroscience of Connecting Brains with Machines and How it will Change our Lives.* Times, 2011.

Passingham, Richard. *Cognitive Neuroscience.* Oxford University Press, 2016.

Rathbun, Ron. *The Way is Within: A Spiritual Journey.* Quiscince, 1994.

Salmon, C. Wesley. *Four Decades of Scientific Exploration.* Foreword by Paul Humphreys. University of Pittsburgh, 1989.

Smuts, Jan Christiaan. *Holism and Evolution.* Macmillan, 1926.

Weiner, Johnathan. *Long for This World: The Strange Science of Immortality.* HarperCollins, 2010.

Weiner, Johnathan. *Time, Love, Memory: A Great Biologist and His Quest for the Origin of Behavior.* Vintage, 1999.

Zahara, Elie. *Why Science Needs Metaphysics: A Plea for Structural Realism.* Open Court, 2007.

Chapter 2: Understanding microchips

Ball, Philip. *The Elements: A Very Short Introduction.* Oxford University Press, 2002.

Blockley, David. *Engineering: A Very Short Introduction.* Oxford University Press, 2012.

Ceruzzi, Paul. *Computing: A Concise History.* MIT, 2012.

Cheng, Peter Lim Tze. *What I Learnt about Semicon and EMS: A Sharing of My Views on the Industry.* Tze, 2022.

Crandall, B.C., ed. *Nanotechnology.* MIT, 1996.

Elmasry, Mohamed I., ed. *VLSI Artificial Neural Networks.* Kluwer, 1994.

Goes, Sanket. *Microelectronics and Signal Processing: Advanced Concepts and Applications.* CRC, 2021.

Malone, Michael S. *The Intel Trinity: How Robert Noyce, Gordon Moore, and Andy Grove Built the World's Most Important Company.* HarperCollins, 2014.

Mazurek, Jan. *Making Microchips: Policy, Globalization, and Economic Restructuring in the Semiconductor Industry.* MIT, 2003.

Moriarty, Philip. *Nanotechnology: A Very Short Introduction.* Oxford University Press, 2022.

Pierce, John R. *An Introduction to Information Theory: Symbols, Signals and Noise.* Dover, 1980.

Soni, Jimmy and Goodman, Rob. *A Mind at Play: How Claude Shannon Invented the Information Age*. Simon & Schuster, 2017.

Swada, Doron. *The History of Computing: A Very Short Introduction*. Oxford University Press, 2022.

Chapter 3: Intelligence—artificial and real

Aladdin, Ethem. *Introduction to Machine Learning*. 3rd ed. MIT, 2014.

Bach, Joscha. *Principles of Intelligence: PSI, an Architecture of Motivated Cognition*. Oxford University Press, 2009.

Baker, Muhammad Ali, et al., eds. *Agile Software Architecture*. Elsewhere, 2014.

Boden, Margaret. *Artificial Intelligence: A Very Short Introduction*. Oxford University Press, 2018.

Cohen, Robin and Bruce Spencer, eds. *Advances in Artificial Intelligence*. Springer, 2002.

Deary, Ian J. *Intelligence: A Very Short Introduction*. Oxford University Press, 2001.

Dreyfus, Hubert. *What Computers STILL Can't Do: A Critique of Artificial Reason*. MIT, 1992.

Dormehl, Luke. *Thinking Machines: The Quest for Artificial Intelligence and Where it's Taking Us Next*. Penguin, 2017.

Evans, Jonathan. *Thinking and Reasoning: A Very Short Introduction*. Oxford University Press, 2017.

Gross, Warren J. and Vincent C. Gaudet, eds. *Stochastic Computing: Techniques and Applications*. Springer, 2019.

Hawkins, Jeff. *On Intelligence*. St. Martin's, 2004.

Holmes, Dawn E. *Big Data: A Very Short Introduction*. Oxford University Press, 2017.

Ilyas, Ihab F. and Xu Chu. *Data Cleaning*. Association for Computing Machinery, 2019.

Jack, Belinda. *Reading: A Very Short Introduction*. Oxford University Press, 2019.

Kubat, Miroslav. *An Introduction to Machine Learning*. 2nd ed. Springer, 2000.

Louridas, Panos. *Algorithms*. MIT, 2020.

Medicine, John. *Artificial Intelligence for Business*. New Era, 2020.

Nachtigall, Werner. *Insects in Flight*. McGraw-Hill, 1968.

Pinker, Steven. *How the Mind Works*. Norton, 2009.

Shalev-Shwartz, Shai and Shai Ben-David. *Understanding Machine Learning: From Theory to Algorithms*. Cambridge University Press, 2018.

Sorin, Andrei. *Software and Mind: The Mechanistic Myth and its Consequences*. Andsor, 2013.

Suleman, Mustafa and Michael Bhaskar. *The Coming Wave: Technology, Power, and the 21st Century's Greatest Dilemma*. Crown, 2023.

Chapter 4: The brain-mind connection I

Ashwell, Ken. *The Student's Anatomy of Exercise*. Barron's, 2012.

Buzsaki, Gyorgy. *The Brain from Inside Out*. Oxford University Press, 2019.

Cytowic, Richard E. *Synesthesia*. MIT, 2018.

Edward, Leon and Anum Khan. *Concussion: Traumatic Brain Injury, mTBI—The Ultimate TBI Rehabilitation Guide*. Edward, 2019.

Elliott, Clark. *The Ghost in My Brain: How a Concussion Stole My Life and How the New Science of Brain Plasticity Helped Me Get it Back*. Penguin, 2015.

Hill, Denis and Parr, Geoffrey, eds. *Electroencephalography: A Symposium on its Various Aspects*. Macdonald, 1950.

Klenerman, Leslie. *Human Anatomy: A Very Short Introduction*. Oxford University Press, 2015.

Porteous, J. Douglas. *Landscapes of the Mind: Worlds of Sense and Metaphor*. University of Toronto, 1990.

O'Shea, Michael. *The Brain: A Very Short Introduction*. Oxford University Press, 2005.

Ratey, John J. and Eric Hagerman. *SPARK: The Revolutionary New Science of Exercise and the Brain*. Little Brown, 2008.

Ratey, John J. *A User's Guide to the Brain: Perception, Attention, and the Four Theaters of the Brain*. Vintage, 2002.

Shilling, Chris. *The Body: A Very Short Introduction*. Oxford University Press, 2016.

Voit, Eberhard. *System Biology: A Very Short Introduction*. Oxford University Press, 2020.

Chapter 5: The brain-mind connection II

Al-Akili, Muhammad M. *Ibn Seerin's Dictionary of Dreams*. Pearl, 1982.

Butler, Gillian and Freda McManus. *Psychology: A Very Short Introduction*. Oxford University Press, 2014.

Butler, Gillian et al. *Managing Your Mind: The Mental Fitness Guide*. 3rd ed. Oxford University Press, 2018.

Braun, Stephen. *The Science of Happiness: Unlocking the Mysteries of Mood*. Wiley, 2000.

Clark, Wilfrid Le Gros. *Man-Apes or Ape-Men?* Holt Rinehart Winston, 1967.

Doidge, Norman. *The Brain's Way of Healing: Remarkable Discoveries and Recoveries from the Frontiers of Neuroplasticity*. Penguin, 2015.

Elias, Maurice J. et al. *Raising Emotionally Intelligent Teenagers: Guiding the Way for Compassionate, Committed, Courageous Adults*. Three Rivers, 2000.

Elliott, Clark. *The Ghost in My Brain: How a Concussion Stole My Life and How the New Science of Brain Plasticity Helped me Get it Back*. Penguin, 2015.

Foster, Jonathan. *Memory: A Very Short Introduction*. Oxford University Press, 2009.

Hobson, J. Allan. *Dreaming: A Very Short Introduction*. Oxford University Press, 2002.

Kolenda, Nick. *Methods of Persuasion: How to Use Psychology to Influence Human Behavior*. www.nickkolenda.com, 2013.

Livio, Mario. *Why? What Makes us Curious*. Simon & Schuster, 2017.

Lockley, Steven W. and Russell Foster. *Sleep: A Very Short Introduction*. Oxford University Press, 2012.

Miller, Richard L. et al. *Psychedelic Medicine*. Park Street, 2017.

Nissan, Nils. *Understanding Beliefs*. MIT, 2014.

O'Donnell, Aidan. *Anaesthesia: A Very Short Introduction*. Oxford University Press, 2012.

Poynter, F.N.L. ed. *The History and Philosophy of Knowledge of the Brain and its Functions*. Blackwell, 1958.

Rose, Hilary and Steven Rose. *Genes, Cells and Brains: The Promethean Promises of the New Biology*. Verso, 2012.

Saxby, Lorie and Phyllis Hiebert. *Secrets from the Brain: Sharpen Your Thinking, Power Your Performance*. Working Brain Associates, 2010.

Sherrington, Charles Scott. *The Integrative Action of the Nervous System*. Scholar Select, 1907.

Torey, Zoltan. *The Conscious Mind*. MIT, 2014.

Zurn, Perry and Dani S. Bassett. *Curious Minds: The Power of Connection*. MIT, 2022.

Chapter 6: Beyond the physical

Augustine of Hippo. *Confessions*. Hachette, 1961.

Ayala, Francisco J. *Am I a Monkey? Six Big Questions About Evolution*. Johns Hopkins, 2010.

Ball, Philip. *Flow: Nature's Patterns: A Tapestry in Three Parts*. Oxford University Press, 2009.

Bauman, Andrew. *Wholeness: How the Love of God Changes Us*. NavPress, 2018.

Benson, Herbert. *Timeless Healing: The Power and Biology of Belief*. Fireside, 1997.

Blackmore, Susan. *Consciousness: A Very Short Introduction*. Oxford University Press, 2005.

Bucaille, Maurice. *What is the Origin of Man?* Seghers, (1976) 1983.

Bucket, Richard Maurice, ed. *Cosmic Consciousness: A Study in the Evolution of the Human Mind*. Innes, 1905.

Burckhardt, Titus. *Alchemy: Science of the Cosmos, Science of the Soul*. Suhail, 1967.

Charlesworth, Brian and Charlesworth, Deborah. *Evolution: A Very Short Introduction*. Oxford University Press, 2003.

Cook, Joanna. *Making a Mindful Nation: Mental Health Governance in the Twenty-First Century*. Princeton, 2023.

Coulmas, Florian. *Identity: A Very Short Introduction*. Oxford University Press, 2019.

Crawford, Matthew. *The World Beyond Your Head: On Becoming an Individual in the Time of Distraction*. Penguin, 2015.

Descartes, René. *Discourse on Method and Meditations on First Philosophy*. David Weissman, ed. Yale, 1996.

Dingman, Marc. *Bizarre: The Most Peculiar Cases of Human Behavior and What They Tell Us About How the Brain Works*. Brealey, 2023.

Dyer, Wayne W. *The Power of Intention: Learning to Co-Create Your World Your Way*. Hay House, 2004.

Eagleman, David. *The Brain: The Story of You*. Vintage, 2015.

Eagleton, Terry. *The Meaning of Life: A Very Short Introduction*. Oxford University Press, 2007.

Einstein, Albert. *The World as I see It*. Snowball, 2014.

Elmasry, Mohamed. *Spiritual Fitness for Life: A Social Engineering Approach*. Pandora, 2004.

Field, Rashad. *The Alchemy of the Heart*. Element, 1990.

Franck, Adolphus. *The Kabbalah: The Religious Philosophy of the Hebrews*. Citadel, 1979.

Frankl, Viktor E. *Man's Search for Meaning*. Beacon, 1959.

Frayn, Michael. *Plays: Copenhagen, Democracy, Afterlife*. Bloomsbury, 2010.

Freud, Sigmund. *Civilization and Discontent*. Norton, 1961.

Giuliani, Luigi. *The Religious Sense*. McGill, 1997.

Guénon, René. *The Reign of Quantity and the Signs of the Times*. Munshiram Manoharial, 1953.

Haeri, Shaykh Fadhlalla. *The Journey of the Self: A Sufi Guide to Personality*. Harper, 1989.

Haque, Amber and Yasien Mohamed eds. Psychology of Personality: Islamic Perspectives. International Association of Islamic Psychology, 2022.

Hall, Stephen S. *Wisdom: From Philosophy to Neuroscience*. Vintage, 2011.

Halpern, Sue. *Four Wings and a Prayer: Caught in the Mystery of the Monarch Butterfly*. Weidenfeld & Nicolson, 2001.

Heffernan, Margaret. *Willful Blindness: Why We Ignore the Obvious at Our Peril*. Bloomsbury, 2011.

Hick, John. *The New Frontier of Religion and Science: Religious Experience, Neuroscience and the Transcendent*. Palgrave, 2010.

Hick, John. *Disputed Questions in Theology and the Philosophy of Religion*. Yale, 1993.

Holland, John H. *Complexity: A Very Short Introduction*. Oxford University Press, 2014.

Hull, R.F.C. and A.S.B. Glover. *Aurora Consurgens: A Document Attributed to Thomas Aquinas on the Problem of Opposites in Alchemy*. Inner City, 2000.

Huxley, Aldous. *Brave New World*. Introduction by Margaret Atwood. Random, 2007.

Huxley, Aldous. *The Divine Within: Selected Writings on Enlightenment*. Harper, 1992.

Huxley, Julian. *The Struggle for Life: The Living Thoughts of Darwin*. Fawcett, 1959.

Huxley, Julian. *Religion without Revelation*. Mentor, 1927.

Izzo, John. *The Five Secrets You Must Discover Before You Die*. BK, 2008.

Jacks, L.P. *Religious Perplexities*. Hodder & Stoughton, 1922.

Kesavan, H.K. *Science and Spirituality: A Hindu Perspective*. AuthorHouse, 2003.

Kupperman, Joel J. *Philosophy: The Fundamental Problems*. St. Martin's, 1978.

Lanza, Robert and Bob Berman. *Beyond Biocentrism: Rethinking Time, Space, Consciousness, and the Illusion of Death*. BenBella, 2016.

LeDoux, Joseph. *The Emotional Brain: The Mysterious Underpinnings of Emotional Life*. Touchstone, 1998.

Le Fanu, James. *Why Us? How Science Rediscovered the Mystery of Ourselves*. Harper, 2010.

Lings, Martin. *Symbol and Archetype: A Study of the Meaning of Existence*. Fons Vitae, 2006.

Mahony, Kathleen. *Simple Wisdom: Shaker Sayings, Poems, and Songs*. Penguin, 1993.

May, Gerald G. *Care of Mind, Care of Sprit: A Psychiatrist Explores Spiritual Direction*. Harper, 1982.

McGrath, Alister. *The Big Question: Why We Can't Stop Talking About Science, Faith, and God*. St. Martin's, 2015.

Merton, Thomas. *The New Man*. Abbey of Gethsemane, 1961.

Mitchell, Roy. *The Exile of the Soul*. Blavatsky, 1981.

Moore, Thomas. *Meditations*. Harper, 1994.

Morowitz, Harold I. *The Emergence of Everything: How the World Became Complex*. Oxford University Press, 2002.

Moses, Maimonides. Guide for the Perplexed. Digireads.dot.com, 2018.

Niequist, Aaron. *The Eternal Current: How a Practice-Based Faith Can Save Us from Drowning*. Waterbrook, 2018.

Passingham, Richard. *What is Special About the Human Brain?* Oxford University Press, 2008.

Peers, E. Allison. *Dark Night of the Soul: A Classic in the Literature of Mysticism by St. John of the Cross*. Image, 1959.

Pink, Thomas. *Free Will: A Very Short Introduction*. Oxford University Press, 2004.

Proctor, Robert W. and E.J. Capaldi. *Why Science Matters: Understanding the Methods of Psychological Research*. Blackwell, 2006.

Richardson, Alan. *Religion in Contemporary Debate*. SCM, 1966.

Rigden, John S. *Einstein: 1905, the Standard of Greatness*. Harvard, 2005.

Rowlands, Mark. *The New Science of the Mind: From Extended Mind to Embodied Phenomenology*. MIT, 2013.

Rowlands, Mark. *Animals Like Us*. Verso, 2002.

Rowlands, Mark. *The Nature of Consciousness*. Cambridge University Press, 2001.

Rowlands, Mark. *The Body in Mind: Understanding Cognitive Processes*. Cambridge University Press, 1999.

Ruskin, John (1835). *On Art and Life*. Penguin, 2005.

Russell, Bertrand. *The Will to Doubt*. Welcome Rain, 1958.

Sabani, Meredith ed. *The Earth has a Soul: C.G. Jung on Nature, Technology and Modern Life*. North Atlantic, 2002.

Salvucci, Dario D. and Niels A. Taargen. *The Multitasking Mind*. Oxford University Press, 2011.

Schopenhauer, Arthur (1851). *The Wisdom of Life*. Dover, 2004.

Schopenhauer, Arthur (1850). *On the Suffering of the World*. Penguin, 2020.

Seneca (c. 49 CE). *On The Shortness of Life: Life is Long if You Know How to Use it*. Penguin, 2005.

Sense, Peter M. *The Fifth Discipline: The Art and Practice of Learning Organization*. Penguin, 2006.

Seth, Anil. *Being You: A New Science of Consciousness*. Faber, 2021.

Sheldrake, Philip. *Spirituality: A Very Short Introduction*. Oxford University Press, 2012.

Smith, Huston. *Beyond the Post Modern Mind*. Suhail, 2001.

Tancredi, Laurence. *Hardwired Behavior: What Neuroscience Reveals about Morality*. Cambridge University Press, 2005.

Taylor, Jill Bolte. *Whole Brain Living: The Anatomy of Choice and the Four Characters that Drive our Life*. Hay House. 2021.

Taylor, Jill Bolte. *My Stroke of Insight: A Brain Scientist's Personal Journey*. Plume, 2006.

Tolstoy, Leo (1894). *The Kingdom of God within You*. Kshetra, n.d.

Ud-Din Attar, Farid. *Conference of the Birds*. Arkana, 1974.

Wood, Bernard. *Human Evolution: A Very Short Introduction*. Oxford University Press, 2005.

Young, Shinzen. *The Science of Enlightenment: How Meditation Works*. Sounds True, 2016.

Chapter 7: Healthy aging—a travel guide

Ali, Muhammad and Thomas Hauser. *Healing: A Journal of Tolerance and Understanding*. Collins, 1996.

Bender, David. *Nutrition: A Very Short Introduction*. Oxford University Press, 2014.

Bennett, Jane. *The Enchantment of Modern Life: Attachments, Crossings, and Ethics*. Princeton, 2001.

Bulka, Reuven. *Uncommon Sense for Common Problems: A Logotherapy Guide to Life's Hurdles and Challenges*. Jason Aronson, 1990.

Carrol, Noel. *Humour: A Very Short Introduction*. Oxford University Press, 2014.

Cohen, Elwood. *Alzheimer's Disease: Prevention, Intervention, and Treatment*. Keats, 1999.

Cook, Joanna. *Making a Mindful Nation: Mental Health and Governance in the Twenty-First Century*. Princeton, 2023.

Elder, Gladys. *The Alienated: Growing Older Today*. Writers and Readers Cooperative, 1977.

Gladwell, Daniel. *I Don't Give a F*ck: Improve Your Life by Ditching the Bullsh*t*. Blossom, 2023.

Goldbloom, David. *We can do Better: Urgent Innovations to Improve Mental Health Access and Care*. Simon & Schuster, 2021.

Halpern, Sue. *Can't Remember What I Forgot: The Good News from the Front Lines of Memory Research*. Harmony, 2008.

Hersey, Tricia. *Rest is Resistance: A Manifesto*. Little Brown, 2022.

James, Nicholas. *Cancer: A Very Short Introduction*. Oxford University Press, 2011.

Philippines, Chris. *Ageing*. Polity, 2013.

Restak, Richard. *The Complete Guide to Memory: The Science of Strengthening Your Mind*. Skyhorse, 2022.

Sagan, Carl. *The Demon-Haunted World: Science as a Candle in the Dark*. Random, 1997.

Storr, Anthony. *Music and the Mind*. Ballantine, 1992.

Summerhill, J.K. *Take Charge of Your Life*. Hawthorn, 1968.

Swan, Shanna H., with Stacey Colino. *Count Down: How Our Modern World is Threatening Sperm Counts, Altering Male and Female Reproductive Development, and Imperiling the Future of the Human Race*. Scribner, 2020.

Thompson, John M. *Arthritis*. Key Porter, 2005.

Tinker, Anthea. *The Elderly in Modern Society*. Longmans, 1981.

Wills, David. *Prosthesis*. University of Minnesota, 2021.

Chapter 8: The future

Ashwell, Ken. *The Brain Book: Development, Function, Disorder, Health*. Foreword by Richard Restak. Firefly, 2012.

Attia, Peter. *Outlive: The Science and Art of Longevity*. Harmony, 2023.

Benson, Herbert. *Timeless Healing: The Power and Biology of Belief*. Fireside, 1997.

Bloom, Paul. *Psych: The Story of the Human Mind*. Harper, 2023.

Burford-Mason, Aileen. *The Healthy Brain: Optimize Brain Power at Any Age*. Harper, 2017.

Butler, Gillian et al. *Managing Your Mind*. 3rd ed. Oxford University Press, 2018.

Buzsaki, Gyorgy. *The Brain from Inside Out*. Oxford University Press, 2019.

Calvin, William H. *A Brain for All Seasons: Human Evolution and Abrupt Climate Change*. University of Chicago, 2002.

Dingman, Marc. *Bizarre: The Most Peculiar Cases of Human Behavior and What They Tell Us about How the Brain Works*. Murray, 2023.

Dreyfus, Hubert L. *What Computers STILL Can't Do: A Critique of Artificial Reason (AI)*. MIT, 1992.

Eliasmith, Chris. *How to Build a Brain: A Neural Architecture for Biological Cognition*. Oxford University Press, 2013.

Elmasry, Mohamed I., ed. *VLSI Artificial Neural Networks (ANNs) Engineering*. Kluwer, 1994.

Fischer, Steven R. *A History of Writing*. Reaktion, 2021.

Fischer, Steven R. *A History of Reading*. Reaktion, 2019.

Fischer, Steven R. *A History of Language*. Reaktion, 2016.

Greene, Brian. *Until the End of Time: Mind, Matter and Our Search for Meaning in an Evolving Universe*. Knopf, 2020.

Greenfield, Susan. *A Day in the Life of the Brain: the Neuroscience of Consciousness from Dawn till Dusk*. Allen, 2016.

Greenfield, Susan. *Mind Change: How Digital Technologies are Leaving their Mark on our Brains*. Penguin, 2014.

Greenfield, Susan. *You and Me: The Neuroscience of Identity*. North Hill, 2011.

Greenfield, Susan. Foreword. *Inside the Body: Fantastic Images from beneath the Skin*. Firefly, 2007.

Hawkins, Jeff. *A Thousand Brains: A New Theory of Intelligence*. Basic, 2022.

Hockfield, Susan. *The Age of Living Machines: How Biology will Build the Next Technology Revolution*. Norton, 2019.

Kissinger, Henry A., Eric Schmidt and Daniel Huttenlocher. *The Age of AI and Our Human Future*. Little Brown, 2021.

Matronic, Ana. *Robot Universe: Legendary Automatons and Androids from the Ancient World to the Distant Future*. Sterling, 2015.

McGilchrist, Ian. *The Matter with Things: Our Brains, Our Delusions, and the Unmaking of the World*. Perspective, 2021.

McGilchrist, Ian. *The Master and His Emissary: The Divided Brain and the Making of the Western World*. Vols. 1 & 2. Yale, 2010.

McKibben, Bill. *The Flag, the Cross, and the Station Wagon: A Graying American Looks Back at His Suburban Boyhood and Wonders What the Hell Happened*. Holt, 2022.

Poynter, F.N.L. ed. *The Brain and its Functions*. Blackwell, 1958.

Plotting, Henry. *Evolution of Mind: An Introduction to Evolutionary Psychology*. Penguin, 1997.

Ratey, John J. *A User's Guide to the Brain: Perception, Attention and the Four Theaters*. Vintage, 2002.

Reiser, Stanley J. *Technological Medicine: The Changing World of Doctors and Patients*. Cambridge University Press, 2009.

Restak, Richard. *The Complete Guide to Memory: The Science of Strengthening Your Mind*. Skyhorse, 2022.

Sargant, William. *Battle for the Mind*, Malor Books, 2011.

Seth, Anil. *Being You: A New Science of Consciousness*. Faber, 2022.

Epilogue

Pause a moment

Pause a moment.
Look at the grandeur of God's work.
Do you still remember
the days when you couldn't talk?

Pause a moment.
Have you seen the baby birds
waiting patiently for their mom?
Her hug is worth more than a mouthful.

Pause a moment.
Smell the lilies, breathe in flowers.
See them shy away from sultry Jasmine
but befriend the roses, the red and the white.

Pause a moment.
Follow the wild winding rivers.
Hear lonely train whistles,
on the nearby railway tracks.

Pause a moment.
Celebrate your life;
a treasure worth more than gold.
Give thanks to God you are alive.

Pause a moment.
For soon your soul will fly beyond reach
of all humans and your body too,
parting under six feet of earth.

From *Divine Love* (Pandora, 2004)
by Mohamed Elmasry

Index

Note: Page number in **bold** and *italics* refer to tables and figures, respectively.

Printed in the United States
by Baker & Taylor Publisher Services